'It's play but it's serious play.'
ARTIST, LEARNING SUPPORT UNIT PROJECT

Serious Play

An evaluation of arts activities in Pupil Referral Units
and Learning Support Units

Anne Wilkin, Caroline Gulliver and Kay Kinder
NATIONAL FOUNDATION FOR EDUCATIONAL RESEARCH

CALOUSTE GULBENKIAN FOUNDATION

Published by
Calouste Gulbenkian Foundation
United Kingdom Branch
98 Portland Place
London W1B 1ET
Tel: 020 7908 7604
E-mail: info@gulbenkian.org.uk
Website: www.gulbenkian.org.uk

ISBN 1 903080 04 5
ISBN 978 1 903080 04 7

British Library Cataloguing-in-Publication Data
A catalogue record for this book is available from the British Library

Designed by Andrew Shoolbred.
Cover designed by Onvisual, www.onvisual.com
Cover photograph by Chris Charles
Printed by Expression Printers Ltd, IP23 8HH

Distributed by Central Books Ltd, 99 Wallis Road, London E9 5LN
Tel: 0845 458 9911, Fax: 0845 458 9912
E-mail: orders@centralbooks.com
Website: www.centralbooks.co.uk

Contents

Acknowledgements

The authors would like to thank the Pupil Referral Unit (PRU) and Learning Support Unit (LSU) staff, artists and representatives of arts organisations, and, of course, the pupils who all generously gave up their time to be interviewed for the research.

Special thanks are also due to the members of the Steering Group for their valuable contribution, to Simon Richey, Assistant Director, Education, at the Gulbenkian Foundation for his support and advice throughout the life of the project, and to John Harland, Head of NFER Northern Office.

Steering Group members: Chris Cooper, Artistic Director, Big Brum Theatre-in-Education; John Harland, Head of Northern Office, NFER; Richard Ings, Author and Consultant; Kay Kinder, Principal Research Officer, NFER; Nick Randell, Consultant, Nick Randell Associates; Simon Richey, Assistant Director, Education, Calouste Gulbenkian Foundation, UK Branch (Chair); Ian Watkins, Behaviour Support Specialist and PRU teacher; Anne Wilkin, Senior Research Officer, NFER.

Preface

The Calouste Gulbenkian Foundation's Education Programme first began supporting arts activities in Pupil Referral Units (PRUs) and Learning Support Units (LSUs) in 1997, focussing in particular on support for residencies by artists. We introduced this new funding priority in the belief that the arts had a special contribution to make to the personal, social and educational development of pupils in PRU/LSU settings, thus helping them reintegrate into mainstream education and to undertake the difficult transition to adult life. No other funding body was pursuing similar policies at that time.

In 1997, therefore, this work was relatively undeveloped. Our initial aim was to encourage its wider adoption, offering grant aid that would allow units to set up their own arts projects, invariably for the first time. Later, as the work became more established, our support became commensurately more strategic. We began to offer help for the training of teachers and artists, for the creation of networking opportunities between teachers, and for evaluation and dissemination.

As with all Foundation initiatives, we were aware that our support could not continue indefinitely. In due course it would be necessary to develop funding priorities that sought to address new needs. But this brought with it a responsibility to try to ensure that other funding organisations, in particular public bodies, were also persuaded of the value of this work and were disposed to support it once Foundation grants were no longer available.

We were anxious, therefore, to promote the dissemination of good practice, or work that testified to the efficacy of these activities. We have done this in two ways: through making grant aid available to projects so that, where appropriate, they may disseminate the results of their own initiatives; and through publishing our own resources. At the end of last year, for example, we published *Creating Chances: Arts interventions in Pupil Referral Units and Learning Support Units*, a description by Richard Ings of some 12 arts initiatives supported through First Time Projects, a scheme jointly funded by the Calouste Gulbenkian Foundation, Arts Council England and the Esmée Fairbairn Foundation. The report was subsequently made widely available, both to policy-makers and to practitioners.

Creating Chances is impressionistic, a series of brief accounts that catch the day-to-day reality of arts activities in PRU/LSU settings as well as the subtleties and nuances of their effects. The present study, which has been planned as a companion piece, is by contrast a formal evaluation by the National Foundation for Educational Research of Gulbenkian-funded projects in four PRUs and three LSUs. Taken together, we believe that the two publications offer a rounded account of this work, each complementing the other.

Although *Serious Play* is a relatively small-scale study, it presents a number of important findings. Some of these are of particular relevance to practitioners; others to policy-makers. Of importance to both is the simple proposition that short-term interventions in this field, though often of immediate value, are unlikely to have a lasting influence on young people's lives and life chances. This argues, among other things, for a much greater willingness on the part of funding bodies to offer long-term, sustained support if the benefits of arts activities are to endure.

This is not perhaps a surprising finding; and certainly not a revelation. Over the years other reports have reached similar conclusions. But it reinforces a fundamental truth, namely that young people in PRUs and LSUs often experience difficulties that are not easily remedied in the short term. Furthermore, for many of them, 'short-termism' – the movement from one institution to another, interrupted relationships – may quickly become a way of life. Arts interventions can, among other things, serve as a counterweight to this and provide constancy and continuity for those young people who are most in need of it.

We hope that this report will play its part in encouraging a range of agencies to consider the value of the work discussed here and thus help embed it in the practice of PRUs and LSUs across the country. In this way arts activities in PRUs and LSUs will gradually become the rule and not the exception.

Simon Richey
Assistant Director, Education
Calouste Gulbenkian Foundation (UK Branch)

Executive summary

Introduction

Since 1997 the Calouste Gulbenkian Foundation has advocated and supported the development of arts projects in Pupil Referral Units (PRUs) and Learning Support Units (LSUs) through its education programme. It has done this not just by funding a range of arts projects, but by supporting strategic initiatives with a focus on training, networks, evaluation and dissemination. In partnership with Arts Council England (ACE), it has also hosted a national conference, commissioned a report (*The Arts Included*) and run three rounds of the First Time Projects scheme, with additional support from the Esmée Fairbairn Foundation in the second and third rounds. This small-grants scheme, designed to encourage teachers in PRUs and LSUs to initiate arts projects and thus develop their confidence in this field, commenced in 2001 and concluded in 2004. In 2004, the Foundation published *Creating Chances* (Ings, 2004), a report which presents case studies of a sample of these projects to illustrate the impact of arts interventions in PRUs and LSUs.

Aims

There is an increasing awareness of the capacity of the arts to engage disaffected young people and a growing body of research in this area. However, to date, evidence of the beneficial effects of arts activities within the particular constituency of PRUs and LSUs has been patchy and largely anecdotal. If public funds are to sustain such work in PRUs/LSUs in the longer term, then more robust evidence needs to be gathered. To this end, the Calouste Gulbenkian Foundation commissioned the National Foundation for Educational Research (NFER) to conduct research into the effects and effectiveness of arts projects in PRUs and LSUs. The study was also to consider the distinctive contribution that arts activities (as compared with other curriculum experiences) might make to pupils' educational, social and personal development, to assess the impact of arts projects on staff and institutional outcomes and to audit perceptions of cost-effectiveness.

Methods

Seven arts projects (four based in PRUs and three in LSUs) were included in the study, all of which were funded by the Calouste Gulbenkian Foundation. There were three phases to the research: a retrospective survey of four completed projects; a study of three projects in the process of being implemented; and a follow-up phase, which focused on the longer-term impacts and sustainability of the latter projects. A total of 69 interviews were conducted with pupils, teachers, artists and other significant individuals (for example the head of a cultural venue or arts organisation). Where available, this data was supplemented by information on pupils' attendance, behaviour, exclusions, attainment, progression, and reintegration.

The projects

Differences The PRUs and LSUs in the sample differed in a number of ways, including: status and reputation (within the local community/school); staffing (e.g. numbers and expertise); commitment and capacity to deliver the arts; and the needs of the client group. Clearly these are all features to consider at the planning stage of an arts project.

Motivations Interviewees' comments revealed that teachers and artists had different motivations for becoming involved in the projects, and suggest that these differences, and their impact on project aims and delivery, may need particular attention from the outset. Teachers and, to a lesser extent, artists had a personal interest in the effect that the arts can have on disaffected young people. Teachers were also interested in creating more opportunities for their pupils; PRU staff saw the projects as a chance to expand and enrich pupils' curriculum, while, for LSU staff, they were a vehicle for preventative work targeting a specific group of pupils 'at risk'. Artists were more likely to describe their motivation in organisational terms, i.e. that PRU and LSU work was already part of their remit or an area for future work.

Preparation The degree to which teachers and artists were each involved in planning and development differed across the seven projects. In some, the funding application was developed jointly; in others, it was managed by one party independently. The extent of subsequent involvement also varied from close communication and collaboration throughout, to contact via email and telephone only. Adequate planning and preparation, based on shared aims, good relationships, and clear communication, emerged as key factors of successful partnerships.

Roles and responsibilities Artists were ultimately responsible for the delivery of projects, whilst teachers mostly adopted a supporting role. Mutual understanding of both parties' roles and responsibilities was a key issue. It was clear that all involved should be prepared to be flexible in terms of project content and delivery.

Challenges Interviewees highlighted a number of challenges which arose during project development, including: funding constraints (e.g. rejection of funding applications); issues of communication and collaboration (e.g. no knowledge of artists/arts organisation prior to the project, staff changes within organisations); the nature and extent of planning (lack of time for prior and joint planning); and administration (e.g. transportation and health and safety issues; organising Criminal Records Bureau (CRB) checks).

Benefits In five of the seven projects, a final performance or end product was incorporated into the overall schedule. The importance of this for celebration and closure of the projects was particularly noted and it may be that more account should be taken of this in planning and funding. There was evidence of the value of using external arts venues as alternative locations for learning and this might also be considered at the planning and costing stage.

Impact

For pupils:

Knowledge and skills Most pupils reported that projects had increased their knowledge of the art form and provided them with new, or better, skills and techniques. Often, pupils linked the impact of projects on their creativity to the development of these technical skills and also to a sense of ownership of the tasks they had performed.

Communication Approximately half of the pupils felt that participating in the arts projects had improved their communication and listening skills. Teachers also noticed an improvement in their ability to interact in a group setting. All highlighted the development of a group identity as a key outcome of the projects.

Self-confidence and self-esteem Interviewees emphasised the impact of projects on pupils' self-confidence and the resulting changes in their behaviour. Increased self-esteem was also evident, often as a direct consequence of pupils' achievements within projects. A number of teachers considered the dedication and commitment to project work shown by many pupils to be indicative of their personal development overall.

Enjoyment The immediate affective experience – the 'buzz' – of participating in the projects was frequently mentioned. Pupils gained a sense of satisfaction, of achievement and, above all, of enjoyment from being involved. Given the current government commitment to encouraging a sense of 'enjoyment' in learning, the affective experience of participating in arts projects is particularly significant.

Longer-term effects Despite the obvious immediate benefits of arts projects for these young people's educational, social and personal development, it was recognised that short-term interventions of this kind were unlikely to have any profound effect on pupils' entrenched problems. Although several interviewees noted a positive impact on behaviour and attendance during projects, they thought that this was unlikely to be sustained within the day-to-day PRU/LSU/school environment.

Commitment to education Equally, pupils did not generally consider that their involvement in the arts projects had directly affected their commitment to education. However, many valued the opportunity to be involved in the projects and recognised the commitment of the PRU/LSU in providing this for them. The chance of a break from the normal routine, working in the informal and relaxed project ambience, was also much appreciated.

For teachers:
Knowledge and skills The majority of the teachers interviewed felt that their own knowledge and skills in the art form had improved (e.g. using new equipment and/or techniques). However, predictably, the impact on knowledge and skills was greater for teachers who had participated in the projects in a hands-on way.

Classroom practice Some PRU/LSU staff noted that they had changed their classroom practice as a result of being involved in projects: they tried different ways of working, e.g. demonstration rather than instruction; new approaches to managing challenging behaviour; and incorporated the arts into general practice. Some also spoke of developing a greater awareness of what pupils could achieve and an understanding of the projects' potential in terms of pupil outcomes. Again, the extent to which teachers were involved as hands-on participants in the projects, rather than in supportive or behaviour management roles, was significant.

For artists:
Skills and awareness Artists mostly emphasised the impact of projects on their teaching skills, specifically in the development of a dual artist/teacher role, and in the recognition of a need for flexibility. Artists also reported developing a greater awareness of the issues and needs of the client group; and an enthusiasm for future work in this area.

For the organisations/institutions:
Legacy and funding Interviewees affirmed that participation had left a positive legacy for the PRUs/LSUs and the arts organisations, citing the enthusiasm of centre staff for further involvement in arts projects. However, lack of

sustained funding was perceived to be an enormous barrier to building on this legacy. For the impact of the projects on all those involved (pupils, PRU/LSU staff and the institutions) to be sustained in the longer term, funding beyond one-off grants was felt to be crucial.

Effectiveness

The effectiveness of the projects was influenced by factors relating to pupils, artists, teachers, project circumstances, and the host institutions.

Pupils' preferences A number of pupils noted their preference for more practical or creative activities: they felt they had got more out of the arts project because it suited their particular learning style. The current development of the 14–19 learning landscape, with the introduction of greater vocational opportunities, suggests there may be scope for building on the more practical, kinaesthetic learning style offered by the arts.

Artists' input The nature of an artist's background and personality was often a key factor in success. Pupils respected artists because they were seen as 'on their wavelength'. Key features of artists' skills and teaching styles were: informality; a more relaxed approach; a positive attitude towards young people; and an ability to listen to pupils' ideas.

Project planning The aspects of projects which particularly affected their success were: the degree of effective planning; the relevance of the project content (e.g. introducing more youth-oriented art forms); the venue; timing (e.g. whether a full or half day); the celebratory end product; and having some form of follow-on to sustain and strengthen the impact.

Schools' culture and ethos The value placed on the arts in the culture and ethos of the educational establishments involved was seen as central to the success of the projects. Internal politics within the schools in which some LSUs were located (including the relationship of the LSU with the rest of the school) was also important, as was adequate funding.

The distinctive nature of the arts Overall, the distinctive contribution of the arts was attributed to the fact that they were different from pupils' usual mainstream learning experiences. The arts activities were: practical rather than academic; contemporary in nature; allowed pupils to achieve when previously they had experienced mainly failure and to express themselves more positively; and focused on developing the whole child, particularly his/her sense of self.

Cost-effectiveness Although employing artists was perceived as expensive, interviewees were unanimous in their belief in the cost-effectiveness of doing so, not only in terms of the benefits to the pupils themselves, but also for the development of expertise within the PRU/LSU.

Concluding comment

This study, albeit relatively small-scale, highlights the contribution arts projects can make to individual pupils' educational, social and personal development. Outcomes identified particularly illustrate how learning can be that 'enjoyable' experience to which the current Government is committed. However, perhaps unsurprisingly, the findings do not offer any strong evidence to suggest that positive short-term arts experiences have any lasting influence on these young people's lives. The research highlights a number of concerns, in particular the sustainability of effective outcomes without longer-term funding and/or further investment by the school or PRU. At the same time, a number of key factors in successful projects, for example, providing the time for planning and efficient administration, taking pupils to external venues, ensuring a showcase end product, all have substantial cost implications. It is also clear that, in order to investigate fully the potential contribution of arts activities to the social inclusion agenda, these would need to be a sustained component of pupils' curriculum experiences.

As a new landscape of partnership-working takes shape in our statutory services, and in the arts, we must also consider how adaptable partners may need to be in order to engage with different professional cultures. Flexibility on the part of both artists and teachers has been identified as a component of successful projects and this will have implications for both in terms of the pedagogical skills they may need to develop in order to fulfil their respective roles. The success of these arts interventions occurs not just where funding is sufficient and/or sustained, but also where there is a greater degree of commitment to collaboration, partnership-working and change.

Finally, partnership-working may also hold important opportunities for those organisations committed to funding arts initiatives with a view to improving social inclusion. As the current national agenda and policy around *Every Child Matters* (HM Treasury, 2003) and the Children Bill (2004) reshape services and roles, direct involvement with the strategic partnerships and youth forums being developed by our local authorities could be a valuable way forward.

1 Introduction

1.1 Background

In recent years, there has been a move towards the greater inclusion of all pupils in education, with a concomitant expansion in strategies and initiatives aimed at improving opportunities for those disengaged from learning. During this time, there has also been an increase in research investigating the effectiveness of such initiatives (see for example, Parsons, 1996; Hayden, 1997; Kinder and Wilkin, 1998), particularly alternative provision for excluded pupils such as Pupil Referral Units (PRUs) and Learning Support Units (LSUs) (Kinder *et al.*, 2000; Kendall *et al.*, 2003; Wilkin *et al.*, 2003).

As Kinder and Harland (2004) note, several of the outcomes identified through research into the effects of alternative provision can also be said to be true of arts education, such as psychological wellbeing (including increased enjoyment and self-esteem), relationship development, and improved communication skills. At the same time, a study of the effects of arts education in secondary schools (Harland *et al.*, 2000) showed that the arts can also produce additional outcomes, namely improved knowledge of and skills in the art form, creativity and self-expression, as well as other skills transferable to different areas of a young person's life.

The Policy Action Team 10 (PAT 10) (Collins *et al.*, 1999) identified a number of issues for arts education. It emphasised the difference that the arts can make to the lives of socially excluded young people, but noted the short-termism of much of the funding for this type of work. It recommended that funding be moved away from 'one-off, isolated pilot projects' into more coherent strategies that would allow all young people to participate in arts projects (Randell, 2002). Recent increases in funding for arts projects under national initiatives, such as the Arts and Education Interface and Creative Partnerships, launched in September 2002, may have gone some way towards this. The latter, a four-year government initiative, enables schools to develop working partnerships with artists and cultural organisations in order to provide young people with the opportunity to develop creativity in learning.

Since 1997, the Calouste Gulbenkian Foundation has supported arts projects in PRUs and LSUs through its education programme and, latterly, through a joint scheme with Arts Council England (ACE) called First Time Projects. As the name implies, the purpose of the latter is to encourage PRUs and LSUs to initiate arts projects for the first time and thus develop their confidence in this field. It enables units to engage artists or arts organisations to work with their pupils. Following the initial round, and in response to the huge demand from PRUs and LSUs, there have been a further two rounds of the scheme, both of which have attracted generous additional support from the Esmée Fairbairn Foundation.

The recent government requirement to ensure that, by September 2002, all pupils excluded from school for more than 15 consecutive days receive full-time and appropriate education (DfES, 2002), is likely to lead to an expansion of alternative provision. At the same time, there is growing awareness of the value of the arts for disaffected and disengaged young people, underlined by the Government's commitment to the inclusion agenda and to enjoyment as 'the birthright of every child' (DfES, 2003) However, despite the growth of interest and research in this area (see Ings, 2002), evidence of the effectiveness of arts projects in non-mainstream settings has been patchy and largely anecdotal. If public funds are to sustain this work in the longer term, once organisations such as the Calouste Gulbenkian Foundation have ceased to fund it, then more robust evidence of its effectiveness needs to be gathered.

To this end, the Calouste Gulbenkian Foundation commissioned the National Foundation for Educational Research (NFER) to conduct research into the effects and effectiveness of arts projects in PRUs and LSUs, looking in particular at any distinctive contribution that arts activities might make to pupils' educational, social and personal development. This report sets out the findings of that study.

1.2 The study

1.2.1 Aims

The research had four main aims:

i   to examine the impact of arts projects implemented in PRUs and LSUs, including assessing their effect (if any) on areas such as attendance, attainment, educational and occupational aspirations, pupils' reintegration into mainstream educational settings, engagement, disruptive and/or antisocial behaviours and the acquisition of skills and knowledge in the arts;

ii   to examine the perceptions of all participants concerning the distinctive contribution that art in general (and artists in particular) make to the potential of projects in alternative education settings to secure positive educational, personal and social outcomes, focusing on implementation and the legacy the projects leave behind;

iii to assess the impact of arts projects supported by the Calouste Gulbenkian

Foundation on PRUs and LSUs, specifically focusing on staff and institutional outcomes;

iv   to audit perceptions of cost-effectiveness, and how reported outcomes may have related to the additional resources provided by the Calouste Gulbenkian Foundation.

1.2.2 Methodology

The research had three phases:

Phase One This phase involved a retrospective study of a sample of three completed projects funded by the Calouste Gulbenkian Foundation, to assess their short- and longer-term impact on participants, as well as examining the legacy of arts projects, for example, the extent to which impact had become dissipated or embedded into policy and practice within the PRUs and LSUs (and beyond).

Phase Two Phase Two of the research studied a sample of three projects currently being implemented (or very recently completed) to examine the immediate impacts of projects in relation to their delivery and content. Agreement was sought from these projects from the start that they would go on to contribute to the final phase of the research.

Phase Three A follow-up study then took place of the three projects selected during Phase Two. The longitudinal aspect of this phase allowed a focus on longer-term impacts and their sustainability, as well as issues of reintegration and progression from the PRUs and LSUs. It assessed the challenges of securing greater educational and social integration through the arts by drawing on the experiences of a small number of pupils as they moved back into mainstream settings or beyond.

Data collection Qualitative data was collected through face-to-face interviews with a range of project participants including PRU/LSU staff, artists, pupils, mainstream school staff and other significant participants, for example, individuals with specific (or specialist) knowledge, such as the head of an arts organisation, cultural venue or training organisation. Fieldwork visits were made to each of the Phase One projects during December 2003 and January 2004, to the Phase Two projects in March and April 2004, with the return (Phase Three) visits in June 2004.

The total number of interviews completed during the fieldwork is shown in Table 1.1.

Quantitative data (for example, on attendance, behaviour, exclusions and attainment) was requested from each of the three Phase Two/Three projects for the academic term in which the project took place and the preceding term where this was available. This data was received from two of the three PRUs/LSUs and, where relevant, is referred to in the text.

Table 1.1   **Interviews completed during fieldwork**

	Phase One	Phase Two	Phase Three
Lead teacher/manager of PRU or LSU	4	3	1
Other PRU/LSU staff (including support staff)	3	2	2
Artist(s)	5	3	1
Pupils	12	11	8
Significant others e.g. heads of arts/cultural organisations	7	2	2
School staff	–	–	3
Total	**31**	**21**	**17**

1.2.3 The sample

Projects to be included in the research were selected, in consultation with the sponsor (and participants), from lists of all PRU or LSU projects funded by the Calouste Gulbenkian Foundation, not just those funded under the First Time Projects scheme.

The sample for Phase One was selected on the basis of four criteria:

- duration;
- arts focus;
- project end date (the projects were to have been completed);
- cost.

Phase One of the research included two projects funded under the Gulbenkian's standard funding priorities and one from the first round of the First Time Projects scheme. Two of the projects were focused on LSUs and one on a PRU.

Given the fact that the projects selected for Phase Two of the research were also asked to contribute to Phase Three, the sample for this phase was drawn from those projects that were currently operating, or that had only recently been completed. They were sampled on the basis of:

- arts focus (to widen the range already represented in Phase One);
- cycle of implementation;
- cost.

All three of the Phase Two/Three projects had been funded in the second round of the First Time Projects scheme. This time, two of the projects were located in PRUs and one in an LSU.

As the fieldwork progressed, it became evident that one of the projects selected for involvement in Phases Two and Three of the study had in fact been completed some time previously. This would have made its continuing involvement in Phase Three problematic as the time elapsed would have been too long, e.g. in terms of following the pupils to examine issues of reintegration and progression. Therefore, it was decided to include the data from this project (involving a PRU) in with that already collected for Phase One. A replacement PRU project that met the criteria was then found. However, it should be noted that finding a replacement that was more current was in itself problematic; seven of the ten projects (mostly PRUs) funded in the second round of the First Time Projects scheme that were approached had in fact finished and pupils (and in some cases staff) had moved on, while it was not possible to establish any contact with another. Inevitably, this caused some delay in terms of completing the fieldwork visits.

Tables 1.2 and 1.3 below show the art form, the age range and numbers of the pupils involved for each of the projects according to the phases of the research.

Table 1.2   **Phase One (completed) projects**

Project	Art form	Age range	Numbers of pupils involved in the projects
Project A: LSU	Drama and digital art (photography)	Years 8 and 9 Age 12–14	8–9
Project B: LSU	Craft (designing and making theatre props)	Year 10 Age 14–15	8
Project C: PRU	Carnival arts movement music (percussion) art (painting T-shirts)	Years 8, 9 and 10 Age 12–15	8–10
Project D: PRU	Music	Years 7, 8 and 9 Age 11–14	6–8

Source: *Phase One interviews in the NFER study, 2004*

Table 1.3   **Phase Two/Three (current or recently completed) projects**

Project	Art form	Age range	Numbers of pupils involved in the projects
Project E: PRU	Dance	Years 7, 8 and 9 Age 11–14	8–10
Project F: PRU	Film and music (e.g. DJ-ing and rapping)	Years 10 and 11 Age 14–16	6–8
Project G: LSU	Music, photography, art and drama	Year 8 Age 12–13	10–12

Source: *Phase Two interviews in the NFER study, 2004*

1.3 The report

The report draws on the data from all three phases of the research. Where cameos or case studies of pupils have been included to provide illustrative comment, the names have been changed in order to protect the anonymity of those involved.

Chapter 2 focuses on the arts projects themselves, including the context of the PRUs/LSUs, the rationale for and development of the projects, organisation (including their aims and objectives, content and delivery), as well as any feedback on, or assessment of, pupils' work.

Chapter 3 identifies and examines the impact of the arts projects on all those involved, i.e. pupils, teachers, artists and the institution, including its curriculum. It concludes by looking particularly at any legacy left by the projects.

Chapter 4 considers the overall effectiveness of the arts projects, in particular the key factors or components that accounted for their success, and the distinctive contribution made by the arts to that success. The chapter also explores perceptions of the cost-effectiveness of such projects.

Chapter 5 concludes the report by drawing out the implications from the above chapters for the sustaining and promoting of this type of work, focusing on the final aim of the study, in particular, 'how reported outcomes may have related to the additional resources provided by the Calouste Gulbenkian Foundation'.

2 The projects

As an introduction to the study, and in order to outline the dynamics of the arts projects, this chapter provides an overview of the processes involved in their delivery. By outlining the overall context, and offering a description of the projects' key features, the chapter aims to clarify the effects and effectiveness of the seven interventions. The chapter covers:

- **context** (i.e. status, staffing, and pupil-type of the PRUs/LSUs);
- **rationale and development** (i.e. background to setting up projects);
- **project organisation** (i.e. planning and delivery);
- **feedback /assessment** for pupils (including end product).

2.1 Context

All LSU staff considered their units to be valued by the mainstream school and felt that a positive relationship existed between the two. In two LSUs, staff reported that the unit was very much embedded within the school system. However, interviewees from the third LSU suggested that the unit was regarded more as an 'in-house addition' as opposed to an integral part of the school. Considerable variation existed between the reported status and reputation of the PRUs. Two of the four PRUs considered that they had a good reputation within the local community and referred specifically to the success of their recent OfSTED reports. Conversely, the poor local status and reputation of another PRU was noted by staff who reported some of the comments the unit had received, e.g. 'it's all those mental kids', which highlighted the community's lack of understanding and regard for the pupils. However, staff at the unit appreciated how this reputation had developed given the behaviour exhibited by their pupils: 'they're their worst own enemy really, the children, with their behaviour and their language'; 'they have got no respect for anybody at all'. In the fourth PRU, the improved status and reputation of the unit was mentioned by staff. Nevertheless, it is equally relevant to note at this stage that, despite the negativity which surrounded some PRUs, in all cases, interviewees spoke positively about the working environment within them.

Staffing levels within PRUs and LSUs also differed, and generally, fewer staff worked in LSUs than in PRUs. Both establishments, however, employed a core team of full-time employees (usually the headteacher/manager and one or more full-time teachers) who were assisted by a number of part-time staff. In both types of provision, part-time teachers often included specialist subject teachers from the arts or ICT. In LSUs these teachers were mainly supplied from the mainstream school.

Interviewees from all PRUs and LSUs noted that the teachers' commitment to delivering the arts was high. However, staff from PRUs in particular considered their capacity to do so to be limited and often poor. Despite their commitment, inadequate facilities (including accommodation) and resources were felt to impinge: 'it's just a case of can't rather than won't'; 'we'd do it if we could'. In addition, PRU staff also identified the lack of arts expertise among teaching staff as presenting particular difficulties in terms of their capacity to delivery an appropriate arts curriculum: 'Staff are brilliant, they will turn their hands to most things, but you have to have particular skills to deliver arts programmes.' For some staff, the capacity to deliver the arts was also stifled by the demands of adhering to the National Curriculum, such that core subject teaching occupied much of the pupils' timetables: 'If we had more time to be creative, I think we would be.' The LSU environment revealed a different picture. Two of the three LSUs involved in projects were located within specialist arts status schools and the third was in the process of applying for specialist status. Perhaps reflecting this, the capacity of the LSUs to deliver the arts was generally high and was particularly good in one case where the school had recently undergone a period of regeneration which had resulted in 'excellent' arts resources.

The individual needs of pupils attending the PRUs or LSUs in the study varied considerably between the two types of establishments. Most commonly, pupils attending the PRUs had been referred for behavioural issues (ranging from constant disruption and defiance to violent assaults) and the majority were permanently excluded from school. Some pupils, having received multiple exclusions, were unable to access any school place. In addition, the PRUs catered for pupils at risk of exclusion and those on respite from the mainstream school, although this was less common where PRUs did not have the capacity to accommodate those pupils. Two of the PRU-based projects initially involved pupils from separate sites within the overall pupil referral service. In both cases, however, this arrangement was short-lived due to problems experienced as a consequence of mixing the groups (e.g. pupil behaviour). LSUs offered full-time and part-time placements for pupils experiencing difficulties in school. These could be accessed, on a referral basis, for a number of reasons including:

- behavioural issues (including truancy);
- specific support programmes (e.g. anger management/circle time);
- support during difficult circumstances (including bullying, bereavement);

- social skills problems;
- reintegration (for pupils returning from a fixed-term exclusion).

Thus, a host of differences existed between, and within, the PRU and LSU sample, including: individual pupil factors (i.e. background and need); staffing (i.e. staff numbers and expertise); site context (i.e. status, reputation, time-tables and organisation); and facilities (i.e. accommodation and resources). It is important, therefore, to consider the extent to which these variants were borne in mind during project planning and organisation (for example, artists' knowledge of pupils' nature and needs) and it is to this aspect that the chapter now turns.

2.2 Rationale and development

This section looks at the genealogy of the various projects including:

- motivation for PRUs/LSUs and artists/arts organisations to take part;
- planning and development;
- selection of artists and arts organisations;
- challenges arising during project development.

2.2.1 Motivation

Interviewees' comments revealed different motivations behind teachers' and artists' involvement in the seven projects. These are summarised, in rank order, in Figure 2.1 below.

Most commonly, teachers described their personal interest and commitment to the arts as a motivating factor in their involvement. In addition, teachers from two projects referred specifically to a personal interest in the effects

Figure 2.1   Motivating factors

Teachers' motivation	Artists'/Arts organisations' motivation
personal interest and commitment to the arts	part of their core work
	an area of work being developed
enriching/enhancing the curriculum	personal interest and understanding of the effects arts can generate
targeting a specific group of pupils	
increasing pupils' awareness of: – community and social surroundings – culture and traditions	
working outside the PRU/LSU environment	

arts can generate for disaffected young people. For several PRU staff, the opportunity to provide new experiences for the pupils, and the chance to enhance and enrich their regular curriculum was identified as the main motivation behind their involvement in the projects: 'If we are honest, initially it was about "Let's see what we can find to increase these kids' timetables."' For a number of LSU staff, however, motivation was identified as the chance to target a specific group of pupils. For example, in one LSU-based project the pupils involved were identified as those 'falling-off the edge', i.e. students who were significantly underperforming. In this case, motivation coincided with a drive to improve the GCSE results of those pupils. In another, the group of pupils selected were considered to be at risk of 'going off the rails'. Pupils within this group were identified as showing early signs of disaffection or self-esteem problems but were not, at that time, attending the LSU on a regular basis. The initiative was meant to provide a useful opportunity to target those pupils and intervene at an early stage with the aim of avoiding future problems.

Increasing pupils' awareness of their community and social surroundings (e.g. pupils visiting a local venue that was accessible to them in their own time) and their culture and traditions (e.g. a Carnival-themed project including a day at the local Carnival/Hat Fair) were also identified as motivational factors in two of the PRU-based projects. In one of these, the benefits of working outside the PRU environment was noted: 'We are always looking for things to do with the children outside the building, you know, in a different venue really, just to get them out.'

In the majority of projects, artists identified work with young people and, in some cases, specifically with those from PRUs and LSUs, as already part of their core work or an arena in which they hoped to move:

> *We're very keen to work with that particular group. It is kind of part of our remit because of where we're situated. A lot of the children that we met at the PRS* [Pupil Referral Service] *live very much in this neighbourhood* (artist, PRU project).

For some artists, as with teachers, personal interest and understanding of the effects arts can generate for pupils were identified as motivational factors: 'I have always had an interest in the effect the arts can have on social situations.' Another artist referred specifically to her personal commitment to working with the client group: 'I really have a heart for young people who are on the edge and vulnerable.' A third noted the benefits of such work both for himself and for the pupils involved:

> *I feel very much that working with these groups of young people benefits me, and ultimately benefits them as well, because they can see that someone who was like them has actually achieved* (artist, LSU project).

Notwithstanding this, artists' and teachers' motivations for taking part also revealed some variation. For artists, motivation was more commonly described in terms of value to the organisation. For teachers, motivation centred on pupil-level benefits. Again, the effect that such differences may have on project aims and delivery should not be overlooked. In addition, it would appear that different motivations underpinned PRUs' and LSUs' involvement in projects. For LSUs, comments suggest that projects provided the opportunity for preventative and complementary work with pupils. In PRUs however, teachers' comments appeared to place a greater degree of emphasis on project work, namely to broaden and enrich pupils' curricula. Although both equally valid, it is perhaps important to recognise the influence of such differences on teachers' aims and, indeed, on their expectations of the arts projects.

2.2.2 Planning and development

In four of the seven projects the funding bid was managed by staff at the PRU/LSU. However, in two, both artists/arts organisations and teachers were involved in devising the initial application for funding. In the remaining project funding was applied for and obtained by the arts organisation independently.

In all projects interviewees reported some form of initial and joint discussion during project planning and organisation. Interestingly, however, the extent of this joint involvement did not necessarily relate to any previous involvement in the funding bid and the degree of each party's early and subsequent contribution differed across the various projects. In two projects, for example, the PRU's/LSU's involvement in setting up the projects was minimal. For one PRU-based project, planning involved the unit issuing a project brief to the arts organisation outlining their requirements. The arts organisation then developed a package of activities to meet the unit's specifications. In this case, communication and contact with the arts organisation was by email and telephone only. In an LSU project (which involved two arts organisations), following the preliminary discussions, one organisation took the lead in planning and developing the project given their prior experience with the client group. As a consequence of this, the content of the project, to a certain extent, then reflected the work of that organisation.

In other projects, close communication and collaboration between PRU/LSU staff and artists/arts organisations was maintained throughout the project and involved regular meetings to discuss, evaluate, and review sessions. In two projects, organisation and development were facilitated by an individual with a coordinating role. In one of these projects (which was part of a wider initiative involving three arts organisations and PRU/LSU partnerships) a project coordinator was appointed within the overall initiative to take on this role. For those involved (including other artists and teaching staff) this proved to be a 'very valuable appointment'. In the same case, a seed day and two training days were conducted as part of the project set-up. The former involved a day of taster sessions focused on three different arts activities during which pupils from three PRUs/LSUs were introduced to the artists with whom they would be working during their particular project. Interviewees involved in the project felt that this event had been particularly valuable in terms of being able to determine pupils' skill levels and any behavioural or other issues that would need to be considered. A training session was provided for practitioners from the school and staff from the partner organisations which focused on the key issues around using the arts to work with disaffected young people. A further training session was held for staff from the local museum.

Given the variation between each party's involvement in planning and development across the projects, it might also be useful to consider the impact of these variations on project delivery and outcomes. For example, to what extent can either party feel ownership of the project when planning and development is not shared? Moreover, to what extent can the aims and objectives of the project satisfy both parties' interests when the funding application (and therefore initial project outline) is managed by the PRU/LSU or arts organisation independently? How might this then impinge on the working relationship between the two parties, particularly if coupled with minimal communication and collaboration thereafter?

2.2.3 Selection of artists and arts organisation

In two projects the selection of the artists/arts organisation to be involved was managed by a coordinator/coordinating organisation. In these cases PRU/LSU staff identified the art form that they wanted projects to focus on and freelance artists were selected according to this specification. In both cases, as a consequence of this arrangement, the artists selected were unknown to the PRU/LSU staff until projects began. In another PRU project staff opted to work with a local arts organisation because of the range of resources it offered, 'there was something for everyone there', and the benefit of introducing pupils to an organisation within their local community. In three projects, selection of the artists/arts organisation was based on previous knowledge and experience. In two cases, the PRU/LSU/school had had direct contact with the artists or the arts organisation previously and selection was based on the success of this work. For the other project contact was facilitated by the local Arts in the Community Officer (an arts coordinator based in the Council's Culture and Community Learning department). In this case a number of freelance artists were selected by the officer according to the art form activities set out in the project outline. This list of contacts was presented to the PRU/LSU from which they could then make their final selection, disregarding any art forms (and thus artists) which they felt would be unsuitable: 'It was by a series of discussions and exchange of information that we actually came up with the people that we worked with.' In this case, the PRU/LSU had not had any previous contact with the artists directly, but prior knowledge and experience was offered through the third party. For some interviewees the artists' ability to relate to pupils was highlighted as an important factor underpinning selection: in one case, interviewees described selecting artists with 'charisma' and who they felt would be good 'role models' for the pupils:

The visual artist that we picked was somebody who hadn't done well at school, but had later gone on to change his life and things, and he could incorporate that into what he was doing with the kids, so that went down well (teacher, LSU project).

The specialist combination of skills required from the artists was recognised by some teachers. For one teacher, selecting an artist with the appropriate amalgam of skills presented some challenges during planning and organisation:

I think one of the difficulties we had was actually finding the artists ... and also to pick people who were able to work with challenging young people anyway, people who were confident enough to deal with this and who could offer a degree of expertise (teacher, PRU project).

This issue was also noted by the coordinator of the arts initiative who highlighted the difficulty of selecting an artist with some experience of working with the client group, without sacrificing their expertise: 'What I didn't want to do was field yet another special needs teacher who's good at craft. I wanted a professional sort of crafts person.'

When considering the combination of skills required by artists, in particular their ability to work with the client group, the implications of no prior contact between the artists and PRU/LSU staff become immediately apparent: artists would effectively be starting a project 'blind' to background information about pupils' and the institution's culture.

2.2.4 Challenges arising during project development

A number of common difficulties in project development were identified, which centred on: funding constraints; communication and collaboration; the nature and extent of planning; and administration. These are summarised in Figure 2.2 on page 28.

Funding constraints appeared to be a particular difficulty reported by interviewees involved in LSU-based projects. In two of the three LSU projects, securing funding for the project was identified as a challenge, and presented particular problems in terms of finalising and then organising projects within the allocated timescale. In particular, one interviewee described how the requirement to secure funding created added pressure to 'rush things' so as to ensure it was obtained in time and the project could go ahead. Interviewees involved in another LSU project also reported some initial difficulty in acquiring funding. In this case the first application was rejected and, as a consequence, the unit was unable to work with the group of pupils it had originally selected to be involved. However, a subsequent funding application was accepted and a new project, involving a different group of young people, was set up.

Two main communication and collaboration issues were reported by interviewees. Three interviewees (all PRU/LSU staff from separate projects)

Figure 2.2   **Issues arising during project development**

Funding constraints	▩ pressure to hurry project organisation in order to secure funding ▩ speculative nature of project prior to funding being secured ▩ funding application rejected
Communication and collaboration	▩ not meeting artists prior to start of project ▩ staff changes within organisations
Nature and extent of planning	▩ lack of time for prior planning ▩ lack of joint planning
Administration	▩ health and safety issues ▩ transportation ▩ Criminal Record Bureau (CRB) checks

viewed not meeting the artists involved prior to the start of the projects as a particular problem that left teachers unable to prepare for the sessions and with no knowledge of what had been planned. Communication problems associated with staff changes (one within the PRU and another within the arts organisation) were also highlighted by two interviewees from separate projects.

Negative experiences associated with the nature and extent of planning emerged as a common difficulty across the projects. A number of interviewees felt that projects lacked the necessary time for PRU/LSU staff and artists to liaise during project development. Indeed, both teachers and artists stressed the importance of mutual discussion involving all parties during this process. However, they highlighted the difficulty of this in terms of project time constraints. Administration issues (including: health and safety; transport arrangements; and CRB checks) were also identified as presenting additional problems for project organisers and were described by one interviewee as particularly 'time consuming'.

These difficulties suggest a number of implications for policy and practice with respect to the development of arts projects. The challenges associated with securing funding suggest that attaching deadlines to obtaining funding might in fact be counterproductive to project development and organisation. Similarly, it would appear that many of the challenges identified across projects are associated with time constraints during project organisation. Practitioners might benefit by including time for planning and organisation into the project application, albeit with associated implications for project budgets and timescales.

The added administrative pressure created by projects taking place at an outside venue might also need to be borne in mind during project planning and in terms of overall funding. In this respect, the benefits of running projects within the arts organisations might be considered against the benefits of working within the PRU/LSU environment (with existing regulations). However, this needs to be offset against considerations of the quality of experiences for participants moving out into the community or other venues. The dynamics associated with working with disaffected young people (including health and safety issues, and high staff:pupil ratios) should also be taken into account when funding arts projects.

2.3 Project organisation

The following section aims to develop further an understanding of the overall context, and, in doing so, offers a description of the various projects in terms of:

- project administration;
- selection of pupils;
- aims;
- content;
- delivery.

2.3.1 Project administration

Project venues varied, with four projects (two PRU-based, two LSU-based) taking place within the PRU/LSU (including a residential weekend in one case) and three (one PRU-based, two LSU-based) taking place at the arts venue (although one included a one-day session at the school). An overall timetable which included the days, times, venue and staff was developed in all projects, with the exception of one LSU project, which involved a residential weekend followed by a number of workshops on an 'as and when' basis. In all projects, artists had responsibility for developing the timetable and for the content of each session. In some a schedule of activities covering the course of the project was developed, but in others schedules were devised on a session by session basis. Interviewees from the majority of projects commented on the 'flexible' nature of the timetables and highlighted the importance of continually reviewing and adapting timetables in order to meet the needs of all pupils. Where applicable, transport, school space and teacher time were provided by the PRU/LSU. However, in all projects, resources (and, in some cases, the venue) were provided by the artist/ arts organisation.

2.3.2 Selection of pupils

The pupils involved in the arts projects within the sample were all of secondary school age, ranging from 11 (Year 7) to 16 (Year 11). However, within this range, the particular age/year groups selected varied across the seven interventions. In addition, there were differences between PRUs and LSUs in the way in which pupils were selected. In all LSU-based projects, the pupils selected were not necessarily attending the LSU at the time. In two of these cases, pupils from the mainstream school were selected by their head of year to be involved in the projects. The teachers' rationale for this arrangement was to target pupils who were showing early signs of disaffection. In one of these cases, however, artists offered an alternative perception, noting, in particular, their impression of the arrangement from the pupils' perspective: 'It was like, turn up and you won't get sent to the LSU almost.' Artists described how the pupils involved in the project were being 'dragged out of lessons … so they were coming into it thinking – we are doing something wrong'. A different perception was offered by another artist who suggested that, 'I had a sense there was a choosing of some of the better ones.'

Teachers' explanations seemed to suggest that the LSU pupils would be unable to cope with the workshops and that the pupils selected from the main-stream school would benefit from the additional work. Interestingly, in order to accommodate this arrangement, pupils attending the LSU at the time of the project were subsequently 'relocated' from the LSU classroom during the workshops, leading one artist to question the situation further: 'Why then have them in inclusion units? I don't know why they feel the need to hold on to those kids, while at the same time denying them.'

In another LSU project, only half of the pupils involved were attending the LSU, the other half were, as described by the teacher, more 'positive' friends selected from the mainstream school. In this case, the teacher described how, through this arrangement the pupils were effectively 'dragging' each other forward.

Within the PRU-based interventions, the pupils who participated in the projects tended to be all those attending the PRU at that time: 'It was all the kids we have here basically.' Importantly, in the PRU projects, interviewees highlighted the emphasis on pupil choice in their participation, such that all pupils were given the opportunity to take part, although the final decision to do so was left to them. Within two PRUs, the emphasis on pupil choice was extended through the incorporation of taster sessions into the overall project. In these cases, pupils were given the opportunity to experience either activities from the specific art form on which the project was to be based or a selection of arts activities. Pupils' involvement in subsequent sessions was then determined by interest and was thus on a voluntary basis.

> *What we didn't want was to force people into doing it, so we gave them all a chance to have a look and see what it was over a two-week period and then they selected themselves really* (teacher, PRU project).

Pupils were also asked to comment on their selection and their comments reflected the project arrangements (i.e. self-selected, teacher-selected, all pupils involved/pupil choice). In addition, a number of pupils within one PRU project described how recommendations made by teachers and friends had prompted their initial involvement. However, their subsequent enjoyment of the sessions had led to that involvement being maintained. Pupils were also asked to identify the reasons why they felt they had been selected. Generally, pupils' comments focused on teachers' perceptions that involvement would 'do [them] good' and that they 'might gain something' from participating. A number of pupils referred to teachers' awareness of their personal interests and/or aptitude for the art form as selection/recommendation factors. For some pupils, the privilege associated with being selected was described: 'I feel like the chosen one.'

In three of the four PRU-based projects, both teachers and artists described instances in which pupils were effectively de-selected as a consequence of behavioural issues, either prior to (during the school week) or during project sessions. Risk assessment of pupils in terms of health and safety issues was identified by one teacher as determining, to a certain extent, the necessity of this arrangement. Behaviour was also an important factor in pupils' initial and continued involvement in the PRU-based projects.

The selection of pupils involved in the seven projects reveals some interesting differences between the PRU and LSU environments, as well as highlighting some common issues. Most strikingly, the arrangement described in the LSUs appears to warrant further consideration, particularly given the disparity between teachers' and artists' perceptions of the reasons for selection. What, for example, were the likely effects of this arrangement on the working relationship between the teachers and artists involved in the project, as well as on project content? In addition, to what extent should the element of pupil choice be incorporated into the selection process and what are the implications for project delivery where pupil choice is not a feature?

2.3.3 Aims

The aims of individual projects varied and there were also some differences between artist/teacher and PRU/LSU aims. However, some common aims were identified across the projects, such as to engage disaffected pupils; introduce pupils to the arts and develop skills; offer pupils a new experience; encourage pupils to work together; build their self-esteem and self-confidence; and to encourage them to 'achieve'.

One of the main aims of the seven projects, as identified by both teachers and artists, was to engage disaffected pupils through the arts and, in some cases, to 'get them back on track'. In addition, introducing pupils to the arts and developing their skills in the various art forms was an aim expressed by teachers and artists alike. Several interviewees also identified the projects as an opportunity to introduce pupils to something new, that perhaps they 'wouldn't do otherwise' or 'wouldn't have dreamt of being part of normally'. One artist described his aim as to 'build curiosity' and, in another case, a teacher considered one aim of the project to be 'maybe just sparking that interest'. The importance of encouraging pupils to work cooperatively as a group and to be able to communicate with each other effectively was another common aim identified by interviewees. Furthermore, both teachers and artists emphasised that projects were a useful medium through which pupils had the opportunity to create 'something to be proud of'. In this way, the building of pupils' self-confidence and self-esteem underpinned project aims.

While artists and teachers largely shared similar aims for the projects, some were more likely to be reported by one party only. Several teachers highlighted the opportunity to offer pupils a 'different' or 'additional' experience as one of their project aims. The opportunity for pupils to explore their emotions and feelings was also identified in some cases. In addition, a number of artists cited aims for the organisations which included giving access to, and a 'flavour' of, the arts venues and ultimately, as one artist described, 'to make [the pupils] feel that [the venue] was a place that they could be part of'. For artists, giving pupils ownership of activities and the opportunity to work with a professional were also described as project aims.

Interestingly (although perhaps not surprisingly given the different motivations for taking part), the main aims of the projects revealed some differences in relation to the PRU or LSU environments. For the LSU-based projects, aims most commonly focused on personal development (e.g. self-identity and self-awareness). Within the PRU environment, however, aims were often associated with social development (e.g. team-working) and involving pupils in the arts. A number of PRU-based projects had aims related to engaging pupils in activities that they were seen to be 'missing out on' as a consequence of (i) being out of school and (ii) the PRU being unable to offer the activities itself.

Most commonly, both parties arrived at the aims of the project through mutual discussion. However, in one case the aims were specific to, and developed by, the PRU independently. In another, individual aims were produced separately by the LSU and arts organisation.

On the whole, interviewees from across the seven projects felt that the aims that they had outlined for the projects had been met, noting in particular the positive impact of projects on pupils: 'the students got a lot out of it'; 'the kids all felt good about it'. One interviewee referred to other 'little off-shoots' in relation to the additional outcomes of the project. However, teachers

Figure 2.3   **Main aims**

PRUs	LSUs
to provide pupils with an experience they would not normally receive within the PRU	to reduce/remove early signs of disaffection
to give pupils experiences they are missing out on by being excluded	to develop creativity
to develop pupils' interest in the arts	to explore feelings and emotions
to raise self-esteem and self-confidence	to develop self-esteem and self-confidence
for pupils to work together cooperatively	
for pupils to create something to be proud of/have a sense of achievement	
enjoyment	

in one project acknowledged that the outlined aims had been only partially met, but noted that 'realistically' aims were achieved given the nature of the pupils. Moreover, teachers described the project as 'wholly worth doing' despite not meeting all its objectives. One teacher felt that a longer intervention or the opportunity to do future project work would enable a greater impact: 'I see it as a developmental thing rather than just a one-off.' Artists corroborated the teachers' views in this case and noted that the aims of the project were met in terms of delivering what was planned, but not in terms of the outcomes anticipated. Importantly, however, the artists recognised that the aims were 'ambitious' and acknowledged that their expectations may have been different from those of the PRU staff who had a better understanding of the pupils.

Although, as with teachers' and artists' motivations for taking part, some commonality existed, it is important to recognise the specific aims of each party and the potential influence of these on the arts projects. Note how, once again, in terms of the aims of projects, the disparity between PRUs and LSUs is evident.

2.3.4 Content

The main content of each of the projects (as well as the age of the pupils involved) is described in Figure 2.4 below:

Figure 2.4 **Project content**

Project A LSU Years 8 and 9 Age 12–14	**Drama:** A play, performed by the artists, about a young girl coming to England through which pupils were encouraged to explore the theme of 'the value of a child's life'. Pupils' input into the development and outcome of the story was a key aspect of the work **Digital photography:** Photographing areas of the school and manipulating the photographs using computer technology
Project B LSU Year 10 Age 14–15	**Craft:** Designing and making theatre/stage props under the loose theme of 'a feast'
Project C PRU Years 8, 9 and 10 Age 12–15	**Carnival Arts:** A carnival-themed project which included music (drum-making and percussion), dance and art (costume-making, T-shirt-printing and designing and making headdresses)
Project D PRU Years 7, 8 and 9 Age 11–14	**Music:** A music project including rapping, mixing, DJ-ing, and rhythm work
Project E PRU Years 7, 8 and 9 Age 11–14	**Dance:** Learning and developing skills in the art of break-dancing

Project F PRU Years 10 and 11 Age 14–16	**Film and Music:** A number of taster sessions including music (rapping, DJ-ing, recording a CD, drumming), circus skills, drama/filming and sculpture, from which pupils then chose to continue and develop the filming, rapping and DJ-ing activities during the next phase of the project
Project G LSU Year 8 Age 12–13	**Image and Identity:** A project based on the theme of image and identity. This included a residential weekend during which these issues were explored through music (writing and recording a song), photography, art (paper-making) and drama

Artists and PRU/LSU staff were asked to comment upon how appropriate they felt the projects were in terms of:

- conceptual difficulty;
- physical difficulty;
- emotional difficulty;
- pace and
- adaptability for pupils of different abilities.

The majority of interviewees (teachers and artists) across all interventions felt that, in general, projects were pitched at an appropriate level for the pupils. Due to their individual content, however, some projects presented challenges to pupils as discussed below.

Conceptual difficulty Interviewees considered the conceptual difficulty of the projects to be appropriate for the pupils involved. In one case, the artist noted the importance of gradually introducing technical complexities to pupils and described the benefit of allowing pupils time to feel 'at ease' with equipment and work with basic resources before moving on to more advanced work. However, in another project, the teacher described the project content as 'deep' and 'abstract'. In this case, although noting that pupils 'coped well' with the activities, it was suggested that the project may have presented them with some conceptual challenges: 'I struggled with it so I'm sure that some of the kids involved in it did.' In this instance, artists' comments considered the content of the project to be appropriate in terms of its conceptual difficulty for pupils. The artists felt that the way in which the content was delivered (presenting the story as a dream) was an appropriate means of engaging the pupils and encouraging them to explore issues. One pupil also appeared to have recognised the artists' approach and, moreover, the rationale behind this approach: 'We thought they were making the story up … but we didn't realise that we were making it up.'

Physical difficulty In the majority of projects physical difficulty was not considered to be an issue and, where interviewees commented, few problems were reported. In one (dance) project, however, the complexity of some of the movements and the physical difficulty associated with them was noted by the artist. This was corroborated by a teacher, who felt that a number of pupils found some of the more complex moves difficult to achieve. However, the artist's response to this issue (to provide additional guidance and tuition to support pupils) was particularly commended by the teaching staff in this case.

In another project, involving the design and creation of theatre props, both teacher and artist noted that some pupils were not always able to master the techniques required.

Emotional difficulty In two LSU projects emotional difficulty was a particularly relevant factor given that the projects were an exploration of personal issues through drama. In one, which involved a number of drama workshops, the teacher highlighted the 'thought-provoking' nature of its content. Pupils were encouraged to empathise with a character from the story being performed and, in doing so, 'engage … in deep exploration of themselves through another'. The associated emotional difficulty for the teachers and artists involved was also noted in this case by one of the artists: 'It disturbed a lot of the staff in the centre and it disturbed the actors actually, at the time, because the kids were incredibly open about themselves.' In addition, one interviewee highlighted the importance of exposing pupils safely to such issues, given that their emotional vulnerability emerged strongly in the project.

In the other project a teacher reported having initially questioned its emotive content with respect to pupils' age and sex. In this case, catching pupils at an appropriate age (i.e. 12 to 13) was deemed an important factor in avoiding such problems.

> I did wonder about that because some of the boys I thought might think 'Oh this is a bit too emotional' but they didn't. We caught them just young enough I think, in Year 8, and they did open up and talk about what their wishes and dreams were and I thought the boys might be less likely to do that, but they did (teacher, LSU project).

Pace No problems were reported with the pace of projects, with the exception of one LSU project in which both teachers and artists felt that it was 'rush, rush, rush'. Some pupils also commented on the pace of the project, most commonly stating that they were unable to complete their work in the allocated time. For one, this issue was felt to have impacted negatively on the extent to which pupils could incorporate their own creativity into their work: 'We had ideas but [the artist] said there wasn't time.'

In another project, the importance of establishing and maintaining a 'snappy' pace was identified by one artist as being a good idea, given pupils' behavioural and attention issues, so as to ensure that they were not 'waiting around for long periods of time'.

It would appear, therefore, that although there may be some benefits to working to a tight schedule in order to maintain pupils' interest and, in some cases, to convey the work of a professional artist (i.e. meeting deadlines), attempting to finish projects too quickly may prove to be counterproductive. Calibration of pace to pupils' capabilities seems a key consideration.

Adaptability In all projects interviewees felt that the content of the individual projects could be adapted where necessary to meet the needs of the pupils involved. Artists' 'flexibility' was highlighted as an important factor in this respect, with a number of interviewees emphasising their ability to adapt to pupils' needs and responses. In addition, some interviewees (teachers and artists) considered the artists' 'experience' to be a key factor in this adaptability.

> *We work with people in all kinds of situations, from all kinds of backgrounds, from all kinds of cultures, so we know that you can go in with a set of ideas, but you have to be flexible and adjust them accordingly* (artist, PRU project).

The importance of recognising and adapting to pupils' emotional state was also identified by one interviewee.

> *Each time that* [the pupils] *come in they are in a different emotional state of mind, so some days you can achieve a tremendous amount with all of them, or there will be one young person who has got their own problem and will impede their progress during that session* (teacher, PRU project).

In addition, some interviewees highlighted the element of challenge presented by individual projects and, whilst recognising the value of this challenge, identified the need for appropriate support.

Some interviewees recognised that it was necessary to take certain pupil factors into account before and during projects, for example pupils' personal interest in the art form; aptitude and talent for the art form; self-confidence; and 'state of mind'. The ability to be adaptable is perhaps a key quality for artists.

2.3.5 Delivery

Interviewees considered the artists to be responsible for the content and delivery of sessions, as well as for the organisation of rooms and resources where projects took place at an external venue (e.g. arts organisation). Several teachers recognised the specialist and professional aspect of the artist's role to provide, as noted by one teacher, the 'master-class'. Furthermore, some interviewees (teachers and artists) highlighted the artist's responsibility to build a relationship with the pupils and acknowledged the development of their position over time, such that it became more of a 'mentoring' role.

> *Originally it was to develop skills and to work with the students, but I think it became much more than that. It became a much more personal relationship almost between them…* (teacher, LSU project).

Teachers' responsibilities included supporting both the pupils and the artists. Most commonly, interviewees reported that the teachers' role during sessions involved observing pupils and offering support to artists in terms of behaviour management. In several cases, however, teachers participated in the sessions, which in most instances was valued by the artists, 'it's good when they get involved with what's going on, that's an added bonus', and in some cases encouraged: 'We tried to get them involved.' In one case, however, the artist reported some difficulties with the teacher's involvement in the project which s/he considered to be particularly controlling and somewhat overpowering. The artist felt that the teacher was 'kind of solving all the problems' for the pupils as opposed to offering an appropriate form of support and encouragement. The pupils involved in this project appeared to have perceived this role more positively, describing how the teacher 'helped out' and worked with pupils to 'get answers out of us and stuff like that'. The importance of the teacher's role being flexible to the situation was also recognised by some interviewees:

> There is a bit of a challenge sometimes, where you have to step outside, literally, and let the young people get on with it, whereas at others you want to be a lot more involved (teacher, PRU project).

A number of other roles were also adopted by the teaching staff during project delivery, namely: organising pupils (chaperoning/transporting pupils to venues); organising rooms and resources where projects took place in the PRU/LSU; and, in some cases, documenting the activities (including a videoing session and taking photographs).

Usually, the way in which pupils were grouped during projects was dependent on the activities in which they were involved: whole group activities; working in smaller groups (as per activity or ability); working individually (as per activity or if a pupil had shown a specific interest or enthusiasm); and in pairs. In some cases teachers had influenced the arrangement of groups to ensure that either pupils worked with others they would not normally have worked with or that pupils who would work well together were matched.

Establishing an appropriate balance between teachers' and artists' contributions to the delivery of sessions would appear to have some implications for project delivery. Practitioners might therefore benefit from describing their preferred way of working and establishing the roles and responsibilities of each party during project development and organisation. Comments from participants do suggest that, in effect, teachers also require specialist pedagogical skills to operate in a project-support role.

2.4 Feedback/assessment (including end product)

Regular verbal feedback was an important element of each project and tended to be delivered informally. Artists and teachers referred to feeding back continually to pupils to motivate them (individually and as a group), 'I assess them visually and feed back to them that way', and to review and discuss sessions: 'We did it as an ongoing thing, asked them what they wanted to do and if they were happy with what they were doing.' In addition, a number of interviewees commented on the evaluation report produced at the end of a project as being a useful tool. In one case, due to the difficulties of the particular project, the chance to feed back and evaluate the project was recognised by the artist as a potentially valuable opportunity to discuss and work through some of the issues which had arisen. In this case, however, the artist described how the project had 'fizzled out' leaving no opportunity for a review.

Formal assessment of the pupils' work was not incorporated into any of the projects and, as noted by a number of interviewees, was never an objective from the outset. For some teachers and artists, assessment was not considered to be appropriate given that pupils' progression and development would not necessarily be within a measurable medium.

> *It is about a wide range of progression, because it is their confidence as an artist, it's their ability to accept and give praise and criticism, to develop a different way of working, to be able to work with different people in different ways* (teacher, PRU project).

In a number of projects, documentary evidence (e.g. photographs, video) and/or the end product (e.g. CD, display) were recognised as useful means of assessing pupils, giving positive feedback and enabling artists, staff, parents and pupils to see what had been achieved. In one case a celebration day was organised at which pupils involved in three separate projects could exhibit the work that they had produced, and which also offered the opportunity for positive feedback in an informal context.

In five of the seven projects a final performance or display was incorporated into the schedule. In the other two, activities were developed over the course of the project up to the final session. In one of these cases the teacher described how, due to the nature of the pupils, it was felt that a final performance would not be appropriate. However, a photograph of the pupils was taken for an article in the local newspaper. Final performances ranged from small PRU/LSU-based shows for staff, managers, parents and other pupils to large-scale public exhibitions.

The degree of importance placed on the final performance differed across projects. It was described as the 'catalyst' that inspired the entire project in one case and as a supplementary and unplanned project outcome in another. Most commonly, however, interviewees considered that the end product provided a valuable 'focus' for the projects, offering all parties a goal that they could work towards. In addition, both teachers and artists thought the end product was important in terms of project closure. For a number of teachers and artists, it provided the opportunity to 'showcase' the pupils' work and convey their achievements to a wider audience. Interviewees described the pupils' final performance or display as a 'celebration of achievement', highlighting the value they felt it had for the young people. Pupils also spoke positively about the final product, describing its significance in terms of offering a chance to evaluate their work and giving them a sense of achievement: 'I just feel proud that they are doing something and I am involved.'

Implications for policy and practice

- Adequate time for planning and preparation would seem to be a key factor if successful partnerships, based on shared aims, good relationships, and clear communication, are to develop.

- The differences in the clientele and ambience of the PRUs and LSUs in the sample need to be recognised and such differences taken into account when considering project aims and delivery.

- Knowledge and mutual understanding of teachers' and artists' roles and responsibilities would seem key for effective delivery. It was noted that all involved parties should be prepared to be flexible in terms of project content and delivery. This has implications for the pedagogical skills of artists and also teachers in their support role.

- A final performance or end product appears to have a particular significance for projects. Planning, and funding, could take more account of the symbolic closure/celebration this can provide.

3 Impact

This chapter focuses on the projects' impact on the range of participants involved, drawing on data from the interviews with pupils, teachers, artists and other significant individuals, for example, individuals with specific or specialist knowledge, such as the head of an arts organisation, cultural venue or training organisation. It covers the impact of the arts projects on:

- **pupils;**
- **PRU and LSU staff;**
- **artists and other significant participants;**
- **institutions** i.e. the PRUs/LSUs (including the curriculum) and the arts organisations.

The chapter ends with a short discussion of the legacy of such arts projects for those involved.

3.1 Impact on pupils

The arts projects revealed a wide spectrum of effects on the young people involved, from the immediate affective experience (i.e. the 'buzz') of participating to re-engaging pupils in school and learning. This section draws on the data outlined above and includes, where appropriate, pupil cameos exemplifying these effects.

In order to provide a framework for analysis that covers all of the potential outcomes of arts interventions for pupils, this section works from an existing typology developed from a study of the effects and effectiveness of arts education in secondary schools (Harland *et al.*, 2000). In adapting this typology for the present study, the effect of projects on pupils' knowledge and understanding of different social and cultural contexts has not been included, as, generally, this was not a main objective of the projects. In addition, in order to address specific project foci, the categories within the earlier study's 'extrinsic transfer effects' group (i.e. those outcomes that were transferred from the context of arts projects to other areas of activity) have been modified to form two categories within the present typology, namely, transfer effects (to other areas of learning within the curriculum) and participation and future plans. Furthermore, and so as to address the first of the study's aims, i.e. to examine the effect (if any) of arts projects on areas such as attendance, attainment, disruptive and/or antisocial behaviours, engagement (or lack of engagement), and pupils' reintegration into mainstream educational settings, the typology also incorporates behaviour and attendance, commitment to school education and reintegration as potential outcomes of the arts projects.

Equipped with this typology, the section focuses on 11 main types of impact:

- art form knowledge and skills;
- creativity and thinking skills;
- communication and expressive skills;
- social development;
- personal development;
- enjoyment, sense of achievement, satisfaction;
- behaviour and attendance;
- commitment to school or education;
- transfer effects;
- reintegration;
- participation and future plans.

Teachers and artists were also asked whether the impact of projects had been the same for all, or for just some, of the pupils involved and, if applicable, to highlight any factors that they felt may have contributed towards this variation (e.g. gender, ability, ethnicity). The section considers the extent of any variation and the factors underpinning this. Finally, based on teachers' and artists' perceptions of the longer-term effects of projects, the section examines the extent (if at all) to which any of these impacts are likely to be sustained in the future.

3.1.1 Art form knowledge and skills

Pupils were asked specifically whether they felt that their involvement in the arts projects had impacted on their knowledge of, and skills in, the art form. For the majority of pupils (with the exception of two), being involved in the project was felt to have increased their knowledge of the art form and provided them with new or enhanced skills and techniques. Most commonly, pupils described learning new skills and techniques (such as DJ-ing, 'I can play on the decks now', and music-making, 'we used the computer and made our own sounds') as an outcome of being involved in projects. Some artists also highlighted this as an impact for pupils, describing specific activities and equipment to which pupils had been introduced through the projects (for example, using a DJ X Box). In addition, one artist in particular described how some 'real talent' had been uncovered during the project and, as a consequence, further development of the knowledge and skills of those specific pupils had become particularly important. Several pupils, however, felt that through project work they had been introduced to a 'different way to do things' (such as colour mixing, brush strokes and background/foreground colour arrangements), which enabled them to develop and enhance their existing knowledge and skills of art form processes. Similarly, other pupils noted the impact of the projects on increasing not only their bank of skills and techniques (such as learning to use clay) but also their level of skill, enabling them to produce work of a higher standard.

Several pupils and artists considered the projects to have increased pupils' art form knowledge and their understanding of the techniques involved in specific art forms (e.g. manipulating papier mâché and chicken wire in a craft project). Furthermore, in projects involving photography in particular, a number of pupils referred to an increased understanding of the stages and processes involved in taking a photograph, including 'finding a good spot', thinking about the background and manipulating the camera: 'You know like saying: "Have the camera this way, and the camera that way…"'

For two pupils a greater appreciation of the art form was identified as an impact of being involved in the projects and was also corroborated by some teachers and artists. In a number of cases, interviewees (teachers, artist and pupils) described how involvement in the projects had developed pupils' understanding and appreciation of the broader repertoire of styles within the specific art form. For example, one pupil described how their appreciation of what constituted drama as an art form had been enhanced: 'I used to think drama was just acting but you can make it into jokes and all that.' In another instance, an artist described how one pupil had initially denigrated the art form represented in the project, but that following his/her involvement, s/he had developed an understanding and appreciation of what it involved. Greater recognition of the complexities and challenges within the art form, 'you think that stuff would be easy but it's quite hard', was also highlighted. For teachers and artists, pupils' increased understanding and appreciation of the arts world (including the arts venues and the role of a professional artist) and, indeed, changing pupils' opinions in this respect, 'it did destroy a few myths', was also considered to have been an impact of their involvement in projects.

One interesting finding was the different value pupils attached to these impacts. One pupil spoke positively about the knowledge and skills that they had developed through the course of the project, referring specifically to the impact of this on their GCSE art course. Another pupil, however, despite studying for GCSE art and woodwork, attached little value to the skills s/he had learnt on the project for these subjects and felt that s/he would be unlikely to use the skills again, 'unless going back into the craft area'.

It would appear that the impact of arts projects on pupils' knowledge and capabilities is, to a certain extent, influenced by their existing understanding and skills within the art form, i.e. projects may provide new skills or techniques, or enhance existing competencies. In this respect, projects might benefit from incorporating some form of assessment or understanding of pupils' prior knowledge and skills in the initial stages of project development, so as to ensure that they provide an optimum learning experience for pupils. Thus, and in light of the issues identified in Chapter 2, the importance of teacher–artist liaison during project planning should not be overlooked.

Pupil cameo 1: Impact on art form knowledge and skills/social development/attendance

> **Pupil:** Andrew   **Project:** Dance
> **Age:** 12
> **Reason for referral:** Excluded from school
>
> As a consequence of being excluded from school, Andrew had been attending the PRU for one year. Through his involvement in the arts project, artists and teachers alike were alerted to the 'real talent' and enthusiasm, 'he loved every minute', that Andrew exhibited towards the art form. As a result, this promoted a drive to develop his art form knowledge and skills: 'With a little bit of extra support [Andrew] would be amazing.' Andrew himself recognised his talent for the art form: 'I reckon I have got some talent because [the artist] was saying I have got a lot of talent … when most people do it first time, not many people can do it, but it takes me once or twice to get it right.' At the same time, he associated this skill with a positive self-image: 'I can get some girls.'
>
> Despite this, frustration at being unable to expand the provision for Andrew (as a consequence of funding constraints and family circumstances) was noted by both teachers and artists: 'We only get him once a week and we can only take him so far, but if he managed to get here on a Wednesday evening, he could go even further.' The opportunity provided by the project for Andrew to interact socially with his peers was considered to be a particularly important outcome, which encouraged him to mix with other members of the group. Furthermore, due to his aptitude for the art form, Andrew also described how he was able to help other pupils in the group: 'When it is their first time [the artist] tells me to help them and help them do the warm ups and stuff.'
>
> Perhaps indicative of his enjoyment of the project, Andrew's attendance data shows an increase of 3.7 per cent for the term of the project compared with the preceding term.

3.1.2 Creativity and thinking skills

Pupils' responses regarding the impact of projects on their creativity and thinking skills varied and, although the majority felt that projects had had an impact in this area, a number of pupils reported that they had not. Furthermore, the majority of responses referred to impacts on creativity as opposed to thinking skills and problem solving. Some pupils described how the techniques they had learnt during projects had resulted in them thinking more creatively about their work.

> *When we were ... taking photos we had to really think before we took it, because normally when I take a photo, I just take it if I like the shot, but with* [the project] *we had to think 'Was it good for us...'* (pupil, LSU project).

In other cases, pupils reported that the impact of the projects had prompted a more creative way of working by 'expanding [their] knowledge', encouraging them to look at things differently and to try out new ways of doing something (such as introducing 3D or using different materials, 'instead of making wood to make something 3D, you could use chicken wire').

Interestingly, some pupils related their ownership of activities to the impact of projects on creativity. A number of pupils, for example, described how they were encouraged to develop and put forward their 'own' ideas and thoughts during activities which in turn pushed them to be creative:

> *We were made to think what kind of thing we would like to do. ... We had to decide whether we would have it standing up, or lying down, or what kind of shapes to use. So we actually had to think 'idea wise' of what we were going to do* (pupil, LSU project).

One artist in particular noted how the project had 'opened doorways into creativity [the pupils] didn't know they had'. S/he explained how certain pupils would arrive at sessions having developed ideas for projects during their own time: 'They come in with their ideas to use.'

In promoting pupils' creativity and thinking skills, pupils' ownership of activities would appear to be an aspect of projects valued by artists, teachers and pupils alike, highlighting once more the significance of arts projects that are flexible to both pupils' needs and responses. Furthermore, it would appear that some pupils linked creativity to the development of their technical skills, notably that, as they were introduced to art form skills and techniques they felt more able to be creative. It would seem that pupils' creativity would benefit most where an optimum balance of artist-led (i.e. to deliver skills) and pupil-led (i.e. pupil ownership) activities are incorporated into arts projects.

3.1.3 Communication and expressive skills

Interviewees were asked whether they felt that their involvement in the projects had impacted on their communication skills, including their use of language, listening to and accepting the opinions of others, and expressing themselves (orally and through the art form).

Approximately half of the pupils considered the arts projects to have had an impact on their communication skills, but a number felt that there had been no impact for them. Most commonly, pupils felt that the projects had improved their listening skills: 'I had to listen a lot more.' In addition, some pupils identified group work as having had an impact on their communication skills, in particular the confidence to speak before a group: 'I could speak like in big groups there.' Pupils reported feeling more confident to contribute ideas, something that they did not always feel comfortable with in their normal classroom environment.

Some teachers and artists described the impact of projects on pupils' ability to listen and, moreover, on their understanding of the importance of allowing everyone the opportunity to speak and, indeed, of respecting others' opinions. In addition, some interviewees recognised the opportunity projects provided for pupils to have increased (and in some cases intensive) contact with adults, which was felt to have had a positive impact on their communication skills. One teacher, for example, noted that pupils were more willing to engage in teacher–pupil conversation than they had been previously.

It is apparent that pupils valued the impact of projects on their individual listening skills. For teachers, however, although some references were made to this effect, several expressed the implications of this in a wider sense (i.e. for interacting within the group). Indeed, the potential for transferring these impacts into a broader realm (i.e. other subject areas or social situations) should not be overlooked, particularly given that some pupils themselves suggested that the development of their communication and expressive skills would have some transferable outcomes.

3.1.4 Social development

The most common impact for pupils in terms of their social development was the opportunity to form new relationships with other pupils with whom they would not usually socialise: 'There were people in my group that had been in the school as long as I have been, that I have never really talked to.' A number of teachers also shared this view and described the positive impact for pupils of having the opportunity to mix with a wider group. The sense of belonging to a group was also a positive impact for pupils: 'It was our group, our tight little group.' In some cases this was believed to help sustain those friendships in the longer term:

> Some of the people I weren't really friends with, … now like I talk to them and … we talk and we joke about it again and we speak about what has happened and all that…(pupil, PRU project).

> Some people that I wouldn't talk to normally went on the trip and I've started talking to them after the trip (pupil, PRU project).

Several teachers also recognised the importance of being part of a group for pupils' social development, noting that projects, in effect, gave pupils a group identity and, more importantly, offered all pupils the opportunity to be accepted as part of that group: 'It has become almost sort of like a family, like a little group that they know they are part of.' The impact of this, particularly for pupils who had been selected for self-esteem issues, was noted: '...being away with people, that social aspect was incredibly important.'

In addition, a number of interviewees (teachers and pupils) commented on the positive impact of projects on teacher–pupil relationships. Projects were said to have allowed pupils to gain 'respect' from staff and to have provided a shared experience: 'This weekend has become a sort of code that we can share.' For one pupil, the value of the development of this relationship was noted: 'My art teacher I get on well with now 'cos like I didn't before … I am getting more out of her. So I can get a better grade.'

Numerous references were made, by pupils, teaching staff and artists, to the impact of projects on pupils' ability to 'work together' and 'help each other out', as well as on initiating a sense of 'conformity' within a group setting. In addition, one teacher described how incidental social issues arose during the course of the project (such as health-related matters e.g. smoking), which were then discussed informally with pupils.

It would appear from the comments of interviewees (particularly teachers and pupils) that the value in itself of project work as 'group work' should not be understated. It may well be that the opportunity provided by projects for pupils to work alongside each other and interact within an educational, but informal, situation should be recognised as an important impact, irrespective of other project outcomes. Moreover, practitioners might also like to consider the influence of pupil numbers on group cohesion when planning and developing arts projects, i.e. that targeting larger numbers of pupils may prove to be counterproductive for some of the social impacts arts projects can generate.

3.1.5 Personal development

Interviewees described the effect of projects on a number of areas of pupils' personal development, identifying most commonly the impact on their confidence and self-esteem. Interviewees were most likely to report that projects had increased the general level of confidence pupils exhibited. For teachers, the pupils' willingness to effectively 'step outside themselves' and 'expose' themselves to trying something new was highlighted, as was the confidence they exhibited towards the art form and other 'art type' activities.

For pupils, the confidence to perform in front of others was identified as one of the main outcomes of the project in relation to their personal development: 'He really came out of himself'; 'It has really been a chance to shine.' For some pupils, their increased self-confidence in social situations, particularly when meeting new people, was noted: 'It did make me quite a bit more confident to actually talk to people.' Another pupil (selected to be involved in the project because of self-esteem and bullying issues) noted that, as a consequence of feeling more confident: 'I stand up for myself.'

A number of interviewees also referred to the impact of projects on pupils' self-esteem, highlighting, in particular, pupils' sense of achievement in their individual successes, 'you could see he was all smiles', and in the sense of pride associated with being involved with a 'very positive' experience. Interestingly, several pupils also coupled the enhancement of their self-esteem with their achievements: 'Everyone was coming around and going, "Whose is that?" and I was like, "That's mine"...'

References were also made by teachers and pupils to impacts related to other aspects of pupils' personal development, including their ability to control their behaviour (e.g. anger management, 'I can't remember the last time he lost his temper now') and their attitude (e.g. conformity, 'understanding that a group needs to work to a routine rather than demanding refreshments or a break whenever they wanted it'). In addition, several teachers and artists described the impact of projects on pupils' ability to maintain their concentration and to 'stay on task', often for longer periods of time than they would be used to. Moreover, for teachers and artists alike, pupils' 'focused' and 'hard working' approach during projects was also considered to be an important indicator of their personal development: 'Once they are here, they are focused on what they have to do and they want to work, and they want to work hard.'

It would appear that, in general, teachers, pupils and artists recognised the opportunity that the arts projects offered for pupils to achieve, and moreover, the positive implications of this for pupils' self-esteem. Underlying this, particularly for teachers and artists, was the sense that within the arts projects, the ideas and achievements of everyone could be equally valued. It seems appropriate to state therefore that, given the evidence presented in both this and the previous section (on social development) and in accordance with previous studies (Harland et al, 2000), the current study offers further support for the power of the arts in facilitating the social and personal development of pupils.

Pupil cameo 2: Impact on personal development/attendance

> **Pupil:** Melissa   **Project:** Music, photography, art and drama
> **Age:** 12 years
> **Reason for selection:** Lack of confidence, experience of bullying
>
> Although teachers referred to her as having 'a lot to give', Melissa was selected to be involved in the arts project because of her lack of self-confidence, and because of her experience of being bullied at school. Melissa herself also reported feeling unhappy at school as a consequence of being 'picked on'. Both artists and teachers described how, at the beginning of the project, Melissa was lacking in confidence and self-esteem, 'I think she felt very much at the beginning that her voice didn't matter', but noted that, over the course of the project, her confidence in her own ability grew considerably to the extent that, by the end, 'She was bossing them all around, it was excellent, they were listening to her.'

Teachers particularly noted this dramatic increase in confidence: 'I have just been into a lesson this afternoon where the teacher didn't turn up and [Melissa] had decided to lead the lesson, which is amazing.' Melissa herself also valued the impact of the project on her confidence to participate, 'I got up and I sang in front of everyone and I've never done that before', and to stand up for herself: 'When people used to pick on me I didn't used to do anything, but now I stand up for myself.' Moreover, she also spoke positively about the impact of the project on her experiences of school, 'I've not got picked on now for ages', and noted that, as a consequence of this, her attendance had improved. Indeed, attendance data obtained for the term prior to and during the project would appear to support this, revealing a reduction in the number of authorised absences across the two terms and thus an 8.6 per cent increase in her attendance overall.

Teachers noted that the project also offered Melissa a chance to reveal her talent in drama, commenting particularly on her, 'great presence on the stage'. Interestingly, although her attainment across the majority of subjects had remained unchanged, attainment data for the term during which the project took place as well as for the following term highlighted a significant improvement in drama from a grade C to an A*, which might perhaps be a reflection of her increased confidence.

3.1.6 Enjoyment, sense of achievement, satisfaction

Perhaps not surprisingly, one of the most commonly cited impacts of the arts projects for pupils was enjoyment. Pupils, teachers and artists alike often referred to the 'good fun' projects provided and, in some cases, compared this to pupils' negative feelings towards school in general, thus highlighting the importance of this impact.

All pupils (with the exception of two who reported a negative experience, 'boring, that's what it was') felt that their involvement in the projects had been an enjoyable experience in a number of ways. However, one artist described how pupils were often reluctant to express their enjoyment, 'they kind of almost didn't want to admit that they had enjoyed doing things', despite appearing to be 'getting something' from their involvement. For some pupils, enjoyment of the projects arose from the opportunity to meet and learn with a new group of people; for others, the content, 'it is not just sit down and write', and being out of school were also identified as contributory factors. A number of teachers also identified the immediate effect of enjoyment for pupils involved in projects, 'they thoroughly enjoyed it', and, moreover, some referred to the continuation of this after projects had finished, '[the pupils] were buzzing for about a week afterwards.'

Other affective outcomes were reported, for example, a sense of achievement and of satisfaction. However, for a minority of pupils, their enjoyment was not necessarily coupled with any great sense of either achievement or satisfaction: 'I just enjoyed it really.' In a number of cases, pupils referred to their increased sense of achievement and satisfaction as their proficiency in the art form improved (for example mastering a specific dance move: 'I like it when I learn a good move and I can do it'). Others expressed a 'sense of pride' in their achievements, particularly with respect to the work that they had produced: 'I was quite proud of it ... it had all our names on it and all that, which was quite good.' For artists and teachers, the value that was attached to the work that pupils had produced was also considered to have led to a sense of achievement and sense of satisfaction for pupils. In addition, for some interviewees (artists and pupils), pupils' ownership of activities was identified as an important element of the sense of achievement and satisfaction pupils gained from projects: 'They have got a voice about it and are getting a bit of pride.' For one artist, this enabled pupils to recognise, and realise, their 'sense of power' and 'responsibility' in their learning, through which they could gain a sense of achievement and satisfaction.

The overall experience of enjoyment was an outcome of the arts projects cited by artists, teachers, and pupils, testifying quite powerfully to the fun and fulfilment arts projects can provide for all those involved. This may be one impact which should not be understated, given the Government's commitment to ensuring that enjoyment is a central aspect of children's learning experience. Nevertheless, the extent to which the affective outcomes of projects are able to generate specific learning outcomes for pupils should perhaps be considered further, if arts projects are to be recognised as effective learning paradigms.

3.1.7 Behaviour and attendance

Behaviour Teachers, artists and the pupils themselves were asked specifically whether they felt that the projects had had any impact on pupils' behaviour. Of those who commented, the majority of pupils felt that being involved in projects had had a positive impact on their behaviour. However, the nature of this impact (i.e. within or beyond the projects) and, indeed, the extent to which their improved behaviour was sustained, varied. Some pupils felt that, although their behaviour had improved within the projects, this had not necessarily extended to their behaviour in the PRU/LSU environment. The 'stress free' and 'laid back' nature of projects was felt to have contributed to the improved behaviour that pupils displayed within them: 'It kind of relaxes you.' In other cases, however, pupils reported that the projects had had an overall positive impact on their behaviour, 'it calmed me down a lot', which would extend beyond the course of the projects. In addition, for one pupil, improved behaviour within the PRU was directly related to being involved in the project in that this determined participation: 'I have to behave... if you don't behave, you don't go [to the project].'

With the exception of one case where teachers reported that pupils' 'entrenched problems' were unlikely to be affected by their participation in the project, the majority of teachers felt that projects had impacted positively on pupils' behaviour. Most commonly, teachers referred to the immediate (within project) or short-term impacts on behaviour, notably that behaviour had 'significantly improved' and that pupils were 'not as demanding'. In one instance, however, it was reported that improved behaviour had been demonstrated by pupils for some time after the project, particularly in art lessons. In another case, the pupils' behaviour within projects was particularly commended by the teacher in light of the potential for them to behave badly or 'play' the situation, given that they were working within fewer restrictions than normal. Interestingly, for pupils (as discussed previously) the informal working environment was considered more likely to improve than worsen their behaviour. Teachers also acknowledged the impact of projects on behaviour in the PRU/LSU environment, where behaviour determined, to a certain extent, pupils' participation. Some teachers described the difficulty of not wanting to use projects as a reward for good behaviour, but, at the same time, highlighted the necessity of this approach to try to encourage pupils to modify poor behaviour:

> Although I didn't like to say 'You are not going to go if you misbehave at school', I would never have stopped them going, because they were getting so much out of it. But the odd time, I would just say, 'Don't forget [name of project]' (teacher, PRU project).

Artists felt less able to comment on changes in pupils' behaviour. Interestingly, of those that did comment, the majority felt that pupils' behaviour had not altered as a consequence of their involvement in the projects.

Pupil cameo 3: Impact on personal development/behaviour

Pupil Adam   **Project:** Music, photography, art and drama
Age: 13 years
Reason for selection: Support for anger management

Adam, a Year 8 pupil had attended the LSU for self-esteem and anger-management issues. The opportunity provided by the project for Adam to express himself, 'he really just absolutely shone that weekend', as well as to realise his potential, 'it really increased his self-confidence', was recognised by the teachers. At the same time, the impact of the project on Adam's behaviour and attitude was reported, to the effect that, over the course of the project, he appeared to have matured, 'he seems a really mature, sorted boy', and developed within his peer group: 'He seems very well grounded these days.' In terms of the impact of the project for Adam's anger-management issues, the social aspect, which enabled him to develop his relationships with other students and staff, was considered particularly important, 'he has the ability to sit and talk things through more now', and, moreover, the impact of this on his behaviour was also noted: 'He's not been in trouble for ages.'

For Adam, although his attainment in the majority of subjects remained unchanged, attainment data for the term of the project and for the subsequent term highlighted an improvement in music and drama. Adam himself also reported his heightened interest in drama and described how, since participating in the project, he had been auditioning for a production within the school.

Attendance Pupils were less likely to report that their involvement in projects had resulted in any impact on their attendance. The majority of pupils (of whom a high percentage reported good attendance in general) felt that their attendance had not been affected by being involved. A minority, however, reported that their attendance had improved over the course of the project, during which time they had 'come in more', but that this had not necessarily had an impact on their attendance overall. In other cases, pupils identified improved attendance as a consequence of feeling 'happier' at school through being involved in projects.

Teachers tended to speak more positively about the impact on pupils' attendance, noting in some cases, for example, that pupils were 'attending more regularly' and that 'punctuality has been much better'. Improved attendance was noted in both the short-term (within projects) and also in terms of pupils' overall attendance. For some teachers, projects had encouraged pupils to feel more 'positive' about themselves and more aware of their ability to 'achieve at school'. As a consequence, pupils were happier to come to school, thus, as pupils reported above, improving their attendance. One teacher remarked that, as a result of being involved in the projects, pupils would be more likely to associate school with something 'quite cool' and so were more likely to attend. Attendance data received from two of the three projects involved in the longitudinal element of the present study (for the academic term in which the project took place and the preceding term) would appear to support interviewees' perceptions. The data shows an overall, although variable, increase in attendance between the two terms for most of those pupils involved.

A number of artists felt that they were unable to comment on the impact of projects on pupils' attendance, given that they had no comparable information. Most commonly, however, artists suggested that projects had had a positive impact on pupils' attendance over the duration of the project, notably that they were keen to attend and be 'part of the group'.

Although the reported impact of the arts projects on pupils' behaviour and attendance varied, the contribution of other project impacts (for example, social development, personal development and enjoyment) to these outcomes should be recognised. Moreover, given the references to 'within' project effects on behaviour and attendance, the key features of projects giving rise to this (for example, an informal, relaxed atmosphere) might be noted and used to inform future practice.

3.1.8 Commitment to school or education

Pupils, teachers and artists were asked specifically if pupils' involvement in the arts projects had changed the way that they felt about school or their commitment to education in general.

Few pupils considered their involvement in the arts projects to have had any impact on the way they felt about school, or their commitment to education in general. However, a number of pupils appeared to appreciate and value the opportunities that the PRU/LSU had provided for them, and spoke positively about the units. In particular, a number of pupils noted that projects had given them 'a break from normal lessons' and an opportunity to 'chill out and enjoy themselves'. In this way, some pupils described how being involved in projects had made them happier at school and had made school itself 'easier to cope with'. The opportunity to be out of school, e.g. at an external arts venue, was also identified as an important factor in this respect and one that was valued by some pupils, 'it shows that they're not always doing stuff here, that you can go out and all that', as well as by some artists.

A number of teachers acknowledged the potential of arts-based projects to impact on the way pupils felt about school and education in general (e.g. a 'more positive outlook'). Pupils' recognition of the 'commitment of the school' and, moreover, their appreciation of the opportunity, 'the school are doing this for us', was felt to be a key feature of the impact of projects in this respect. Some teachers also described the impact of projects on pupils' perceptions of how they were viewed by the PRU/LSU/school, notably their increased awareness and recognition that schools valued their opinions: 'They do matter.' For the majority of teachers, the impact of projects on pupils' commitment to education was considered to be ultimately a short-term effect, and it was noted that any longer-term impact would be difficult to gauge. It was hoped, however, that the 'overall positive experience' would have some lasting effect. In other cases, teachers felt that projects were unlikely to have any impact on pupils' feelings about school or their commitment to education, and highlighted their 'entrenched' attitudes towards school and the short-term nature of projects ('they still come back to classrooms') in this respect.

Artists spoke positively about the impact of projects on how pupils felt about school and their commitment to education and, although a number noted that they could not categorically report this effect, many were optimistic about the outcomes of projects. Several artists, however, identified a number of ways in which projects were likely to have had an effect on pupils, most commonly the privilege of being involved in projects, 'having a special project for them', which enabled them to stand apart from others: 'It made them feel quite special'; 'It gives them that sort of edge.' For one artist, the project offered pupils a different way to work, 'in a very exciting, free, and liberating manner', through which pupils were able to enjoy working with others and thus look at their education in a different light.

Whilst they were unlikely to report a greater commitment to school or education in general, the opportunity of a break from the normal routine did appear to be valued by pupils. In this respect, and in line with previous research (see, for example, Harland *et al.*, 2000), the therapeutic outcomes of the arts projects, i.e. offering a release from everyday stresses, should not be overlooked. Moreover, and perhaps irrespective of any impact on pupils' commitment to school or education in general, the sense of privilege associated with being involved in the arts projects, and the effect of this for pupils' self-esteem, should also be recognised.

3.1.9 Transfer effects

Pupils, teachers, and artists were asked specifically whether the outcomes of the arts projects had transferred into other subjects areas, including:

- the way pupils learn in other subjects;
- pupils' interest in other subjects;
- pupils' understanding in other subjects.

Transfer effects: the way pupils learn in other subjects Almost half of the pupils noted that being involved in the projects had produced some general learning outcomes, which had been of benefit to the way they learnt in other subjects. Some reported that, because of the importance of concentrating during arts projects, their concentration skills had improved and they were able to apply them in other lessons: 'I concentrate more in lessons so that I can learn more.' For example, in one physical (dance) project a pupil described how concentration was a key factor of success and avoiding injury: 'If you don't concentrate you are going to hurt yourself.' Several other pupils identified their improved listening skills as an outcome of projects which they had been able to transfer to the way that they learnt in other subjects: '[The project] makes me listen a lot.' Another pupil described how the artists introduced them to different modes of working, demonstrating ways to overcome problems and tackle difficult or complex activities. This had highlighted 'easier' ways to work through problems which the pupil concerned had been able to apply to the way s/he learnt in other subjects: 'Sometimes you have to learn the hard way, but you can work at it easily instead.'

Teachers also reported that projects had had an impact on the ways in which pupils learnt in their other subjects, in particular, that they were more likely to 'have a go' and contribute in lessons and, moreover, that when doing so they were in fact able to 'articulate an issue' more appropriately. For teachers, the way in which projects encouraged pupils that 'nothing was a failure' was a key factor of this impact.

Transfer effects: pupils' interest in other subjects A number of pupils felt that their participation in the projects had resulted in some impact on their interest in other subjects, most commonly reporting an increased interest in the particular art form in which they had been involved: 'I want to do like filming and music and all that'; 'I am more interested in those [arts] subjects now'. In some cases pupils reported an increased interest in other subject areas that had been incorporated into the arts projects, namely ICT. Pupils were less likely to describe an increased interest in subjects beyond the project (such as maths and English). In fact, one pupil reported a decrease in his interest in these subjects as a consequence of being involved in projects, because of an established preference for the arts: 'I want to do [the arts projects] more.'

In some cases, teachers were able to link project content and outcomes directly to effects on pupils' interest within their other subjects. For example, in one project which incorporated a music element, the direct impact of this on pupils' interest in English lessons was noted: 'The rapping actually introduced the idea that poetry could be fun and that [the pupils] could make their own poems.'

Transfer effects: pupils' understanding in other subjects For pupils, the impact of projects on their understanding in other subjects did not extend to subjects outside of the arts. Pupils noted the impact of projects on their knowledge, such as art form vocabulary and definitions, 'I know a lot more weird words', and skills, 'I have transferred a few skills into my woodwork class', in the various art forms, and the impact of this on their level of understanding in these specific areas.

Teachers noted that the techniques learnt in film-making were also linked to pupils' understanding in their media studies GCSE. In other cases, teachers reported that projects had had an impact on pupils' understanding of arts subjects, 'there are definite links to art and [design] technology', where pupils were said to have gained a 'deeper understanding', but these impacts were not felt to have extended to other areas of the curriculum.

At a more general level, teachers also referred to the personal and social outcomes of projects and the way in which these transferred to other subjects (for example, the ability to work together as having transfer effects in subjects such as drama, and having 'something to talk about' as useful in English). In addition, the sense of achievement and the development of staff–pupil relationships were also considered to have had a positive impact on pupils in other lessons. For one teacher the physical approach to project work was considered to have had a 'stimulating' effect on pupils which was reported to have had an impact on their concentration in other lessons.

The majority of artists were also of the opinion that pupils' involvement in the arts projects would have had some impact on their other subjects, although they were less likely to offer any specific examples.

Of those pupils who reported no transfer effects from projects, two pupils highlighted the demands of their GCSE work at the time, noting that this stifled the importance of what they had learnt during the projects because they were 'knuckling down' to work towards their exams and as such 'put [the project] to the back of my mind'.

Evidence to support the impact of arts projects on wider learning outcomes appears to relate most commonly to effects within the arts subjects themselves. The extent to which this meets the objectives of arts projects to generate wider learning outcomes is therefore questionable. However, the potential of arts projects to secure an interest in any subject area (albeit the arts) would appear to support the move towards making education more inclusive. It is also important to recognise the impact of projects on pupils' communication skills, and personal and social development, and the influence of these outcomes in other arenas.

3.1.10 Reintegration

The third phase of the research provided a longitudinal element to the study in order to assess the longer term impacts of the arts projects, including their impact on levels of reintegration. Pupils and teachers were asked specifically if they felt that involvement in the arts projects had had any impact on pupils' reintegration into mainstream school or, in the case of LSUs, regular lessons. However, it should be noted that this was not easy to determine in the current study. Of the sample of pupils from the four PRU-based projects, only two pupils had reintegrated into a mainstream school. Of the pupils attending the LSU-based projects, not all were actually part of the LSU's regular clientele at the time of the project (as discussed in Chapter 2). Thus, questions regarding reintegration were of little relevance for some interviewees.

The following outcomes are discussed in the light of the above caveat. Most commonly, teachers and pupils spoke positively about the opportunity projects provided for pupils to achieve. The resulting impact this had on raising pupils' levels of confidence and self-esteem was seen as a key element of successful reintegration (either back into pupils' regular lessons or into mainstream school). One pupil, for example, described feeling 'on edge' in the classroom environment, in case s/he was asked to participate or answer a question. In this instance, the pupil described feeling more relaxed in the project situation, as well as more willing to become involved in project and subsequent activities as a consequence of the increased confidence s/he had gained through participating in the arts project. For one teacher, the opportunity offered by projects for pupils to engage in a hands-on, practical activity was particularly commended, given the difficulties for some pupils with numeracy and literacy: 'If they find they are good at the practical things ... then, if they go to school they know there is going to be something they are going to be good at.' For teachers the development of pupils' communication skills through projects (for example, being able to talk things through with teaching staff and to assert themselves in a non-aggressive manner) was also considered to be of importance in terms of reintegration. Furthermore, teachers referred to the impact of projects on pupils' social skills (such as working together) as being influential in the reintegration process.

Although the impact of the arts projects on pupils' reintegration has proved somewhat difficult to determine through the present study, their contribution to the development of pupils' personal and social well-being, and the subsequent influence of this on reintegration is duly noted.

3.1.11 Participation and future plans

Pupils, teachers and artists were asked specifically whether the arts projects had impacted on pupils' future participation in the art form (including leisure and/or extracurricular activities), or on their career plans.

Participation in the art form In the majority of projects, pupils did not report that their involvement had had any impact on their participation in the art form outside of school, for example, in their leisure activities. Most commonly, pupils described their participation in the art form outside school in terms of showing what they had learnt to friends and family, for example, through personal performances: 'We do dances for our parents and all that.' A number of pupils also described how they would 'practice' and 'go over and over it again at home'. Interestingly, in this case, teachers described how the PRU had bought some resources to enable pupils to practice there too. In addition, two pupils had in fact taken up the art form as a leisure pursuit and were attending lessons in their own time, while another pupil had been involved in a dance production at a local school. Other pupils spoke in terms of a broader impact on their participation, for example, 'doing more art work', or referred to specific instances of art form participation, for example, using a camera with the family.

In one particularly successful PRU-based project, a number of pupils and teachers involved noted various impacts of the project on the pupils' participation in the art form outside school. Interestingly, the teachers described how the PRU was hoping to secure some extended funding to be able to support particularly talented pupils in their continued participation.

Generally, however, teachers tended to speak less positively, commenting that it was unlikely that pupils would become involved in the art form in their extracurricular or out-of-school activities. In particular, teachers noted that pupils often did little outside of school anyway; they were often 'socially excluded' and so felt restricted in what they could do, and, moreover, in their own time 'did not want to know anything about school'. Where teachers did refer to pupils' increased interest in arts activities, it was usually in more general terms, they 'dabbled in it', or through extracurricular activities such as, for example, joining a local steel band or auditioning for school drama and dance productions.

Artists spoke more positively about the impact of the projects on pupils' participation in the art form. The majority felt that pupils' involvement in projects had sparked an interest, which might increase future participation, for example, the chance that pupils might 'pop in' to a museum. Various artists expressed some frustration at the difficulties pupils had in accessing the art form in their own time: 'They want to come here in the evenings but can't get here, literally cannot get here'; 'They go home to their parents and it is out of our hands.'

At this stage, it is important to point out that, although projects were considered to have made a noteworthy contribution to pupils' interest and, in some cases, increased participation in the various art forms, they were unable to provide the additional support required to sustain or extend these impacts. In addition, the numerous personal factors that would also affect pupils' ability to participate (such as family circumstances, social exclusion, and financial issues) should also be considered when evaluating the impact of projects on pupils' participation in the art form. It would seem, therefore, that whilst projects may spark an interest for many pupils and offer them opportunities, sustained support to address the numerous factors which hinder pupils' participation would be required in order to capitalise on their enthusiasm and extend impact beyond the arts projects themselves.

Future plans Pupils rarely considered projects to have had any impact on their future plans, particularly career plans, and in many cases, pupils tended to reference existing career aspirations (e.g. professional golfer, working with animals, mechanic, chef). For some pupils, however, their involvement in projects corresponded to their career aspirations (such as to be an actress or dancer) and for others had provided ideas and insights into different career possibilities. Nevertheless, one pupil reported a direct impact of the project on his/her future plans to access an Audio Media college course. The content of the project, 'it was like a little media course', was felt to have influenced this decision.

Teachers and artists spoke positively about the impact of projects on pupils' future plans. However, comments tended to be optimistic in this respect, referring more to the potential of projects, 'it would give him an interest in life', rather than any actual impact. Even so, in some cases, interviewees reported a project–career link for some pupils, including working in a museum and becoming a dancer. Once again the issue of further support to enable pupils to realise their ambitions was raised:

> She said she wanted to be a dancer … with having that outside activity as well it could become an option, but [the pupils] are never really getting the chance to realise how much further they could go (artist, PRU project).

Interestingly, and in addition to the effects discussed above, teachers highlighted the commitment, 'we have got those kids involved, who have turned up just about every single week for the sessions', enthusiasm and dedication, 'they put everything they'd got into it', shown by pupils involved in some projects, noting that this in itself should be recognised as a considerable achievement.

The potential impact of projects on pupils' future participation in the arts and/or career plans, although ultimately dependent on their interests, would appear to have certain implications for project funding. Although one-off or short-term projects would seem able to inspire and interest some pupils, the extent to which this interest can then be sustained and developed without the aid of further funding is questionable, and should perhaps be an area for consideration in terms of the way in which the funding of arts projects might be advanced.

3.1.12 Variation of impact

As might be expected, interviewees reported that the impact of the projects had not been the same for all pupils, noting in several cases the likelihood of this given the effect of group dynamics. In all cases, interviewees considered projects to have had a positive impact on pupils, albeit in different ways, 'they all got different kinds of things out of it', and to varying degrees: 'Some have gained more than others but they have all gained.' A number of factors were attributed to this variation, most commonly individual pupil factors, including, personality, personal interest, circumstance and needs. For some interviewees, 'the very nature of the pupils themselves' was considered to have contributed to the variation of pupil impact. Resistance to becoming involved with projects was identified as one issue in this respect and, in a number of cases, was linked to the peer pressure that existed within the group. One teacher noted, for example:

> I think it was more of a teenage thing of, 'My friend is here and I can't completely let go or let somebody else take control.' They were a bit loathe to get 100 per cent involved, because they were standing shoulder to shoulder, joined at the hip kind of thing (teacher, LSU project).

For this reason, the logistics of the group was identified as an important factor in terms of the selection of pupils. Personal interest and aptitude for the art form were also considered to be factors that contributed to the variation of impact for pupils: 'It's not going to work for everybody, it's going to be right for some kids.' In addition, a number of interviewees identified the influence of pupils' individual backgrounds, 'the world [they] lived in', or particular circumstances, 'what happened to them that morning, what happened to them the night before', as contributing to the variation of impact. The specific and individual needs that pupils brought to projects were also recognised by some interviewees, for example, one teacher described the 'continuum of need' within the group and noted the influence of this on the impact of the project for specific pupils.

Pupil attendance (which enabled pupils to develop deeper involvement and understanding), as well as gender (for example, where all-male groups would 'play up' to each other), were identified as influential factors for project impact in some cases. Interviewees also highlighted project factors as contributing to the variation of impact for pupils involved, including, finding some aspects of projects more enjoyable or agreeable than others, 'it's about finding their particular niche that they can develop and be good at'; project organisation and delivery, such as high staff to pupil ratio, '[the pupils] spent a lot of time with lots of different people'; or, as noted by one teacher, their experience of the projects in general: 'With anything that's arts, it's about how you perceive it isn't it, and how you experience it.'

Although highlighting the variation of impact among pupils, this section offers support for the positive impact (albeit to different degrees) of the arts for disaffected young people. Furthermore, it identifies the influence of factors relating to individual pupils (e.g. personality, personal interest, circumstances and needs) on the effects that the arts projects can generate and, in so doing, stresses the importance of taking these factors into consideration during project development.

3.1.13 Longer-term impacts

Teachers and artists were optimistic about the longer-term impacts of projects, although they were unlikely to identify specific long-term outcomes. For teachers and artists alike, the 'positive experience' offered by projects was considered to be an important feature which would be likely to have longer-term impacts for pupils, for example, pupils would be able to 'look back' on or be 'reminded' of the experience. Moreover, the positive long-term impact of the projects on pupils' achievement, 'it is one thing they can feel they can be really, really good at', was also considered to be of particular importance and would 'ultimately give them the confidence and the ability to go on and do whatever they want to do'.

The effect on pupils' social development generally was considered to have benefits for pupils in the longer term. More specifically, the development of the pupils' relationships with the teaching staff was identified as an impact that might possibly benefit both the pupils themselves and the teaching staff in the future, for example, as a 'good lever' to remind pupils of their achievement. In other cases, interviewees described the longer-term impact of projects on pupils' increased interest in the art form, or likelihood of visiting the arts venue, in the future.

Given the fact that interviewees considered the projects to be a positive experience for pupils to look back on, or be reminded of, it may be useful to consider, in terms of project organisation and funding, ways in which the memory of the arts projects could be sustained for pupils, for example, through additional funding to support the provision of follow-up project work.

3.2 Impact on PRU and LSU staff

This section considers the impact on staff from the PRUs and LSUs who were involved in the arts projects. It draws on data from the interviews conducted with PRU/LSU staff themselves, artists and other significant participants, for example, individuals with specific (or specialist) knowledge, such as the head of an arts organisation, cultural venue or training organisation. The section focuses on six main types of impact:

- art form knowledge and skills;
- impact on practice;
- therapeutic and affective outcomes;
- new or increased awareness;

- attitudinal and motivational outcomes;
- informational outcomes.

The above range of impacts was adapted from a typology of continuing professional development (CPD) outcomes devised by Harland and Kinder (1997).

3.2.1 Art form knowledge and skills

Interviewees were specifically asked whether teachers' involvement in the arts project had impacted on their knowledge of, and skills in, the art form. The majority of teachers and artists felt that it had, although the degree of impact appeared to differ according to teachers' familiarity with the arts focus of the project and the extent of hands-on involvement they had. For example, in two of the music-focused projects even those teachers with a musical bent reported learning new techniques and gaining experience in using musical equipment (such as a DJ X box). As the projects progressed, artists noted a change towards more professional terminology when teachers were describing the equipment. In a third project with a music focus the impact was said to be limited because teachers had not been 'hands on'. Similarly, in a dance project the impact on teachers' knowledge or skills in the art form was said to be greater for those who had participated. In fact, their participation had led to one of the staff going on to take up dance lessons with the organisation involved.

For the projects with an arts/craft focus teachers were less clear about an impact on their art form knowledge and skills: 'It was just stuff I'd done before.' However, despite a feeling of familiarity with the art form, again it was apparent that where teachers had been more involved in the practical activities their skills and knowledge of art/craft techniques were felt to have improved: 'This is so simple, I am going to do this with my kids', and 'I hadn't thought of doing it like that before.' Thus, although they might use art and craft techniques in their work, teachers were now believed to be extending their skills, and looking at alternative methods or ideas to use in their teaching of the art form.

> We're doing a lot of weaving and printing everything now with the lino prints, so everything like that, everything that we were using in the project, we are now using in art (teacher, PRU project).

It would appear then, that the development of both teachers' knowledge or skills of the art from and their teaching of it depended to a large extent on the degree to which they had been a hands-on participant, rather than being present in a supportive, or behaviour management role. The issue of teacher involvement may well have important implications for policy and practice.

> It's a process. We are taking the kids through a process, so unless you are part of observing that process and are really engaged in how the kids are

functioning within that it is difficult to understand what we are doing
(artist, LSU project).

3.2.2 Impact on practice

PRU/LSU staff reported an impact on their general classroom practice as a result of being involved in the arts projects. For some teachers seeing other professionals working successfully in different ways with the young people had enabled them to use the same techniques (e.g. demonstration as opposed to instruction, more adult ways of interacting) in their other lessons. For example, in two projects that focused on film and digital photography the artists had demonstrated how to use the equipment (cameras, and computers to edit or manipulate images) and then the pupils had been trusted to go off on their own to use it. The success of this exercise was felt to have shown the teaching staff involved just what pupils could achieve and how they could manage tasks with the minimum of instruction and guidance.

Artists' approaches to managing challenging behaviour were perceived to be particularly influential for teachers. Such techniques were believed to be easily transferable to other areas of their teaching practice.

> *It's seeing the different ways that people who aren't teachers work with children to get them to do something that they want them to do, that the children don't want to do in the first place* (teacher, LSU project).

After observing a session involving role play, one teaching assistant spoke about successfully using this technique in circle-time activities with pupils to address anger management issues. However, one artist did note that there was a limit to how far teachers could stretch the level of informality adopted by artists when working with the young people on a day-to-day basis over a longer period of time. It was felt that being too informal could have a detrimental effect when wanting to 'rein them in'.

3.2.3 Therapeutic and affective outcomes

A number of therapeutic or affective outcomes for PRU/LSU staff were noted. Staff themselves spoke of how much they had enjoyed the experience and reported feeling a sense of pride, sometimes accompanied by surprise, in seeing what the pupils could achieve.

> *I think a lot of people felt quite emotional about what the children came up with, very proud of what they had dared to think about. And they did come up with very ambitious targets for themselves* (teacher, LSU project).

> *It was really seeing the children in the project itself and seeing what they got out of it in the process, then listening to the CD, watching the exhibition go up and just the little glow on their faces really* (teacher, LSU project).

PRU/LSU staff had also benefited in terms of strengthened relationships with the artists and with the young people involved, through watching them interact with other adults in different settings. Seeing what other professionals could bring out of the young people was reported to have strengthened the respect that some staff had for the artists. As a result, it was believed teachers would feel more confident about working with pupils in this way in the future, for example, working in groups more or visiting arts venues.

Artists from two of the projects highlighted the beneficial effect for teachers of having an outside person coming in to work with the pupils in terms of relieving some of the pressure on them: 'It gives them something to enthuse about with the kids and gives them a bit of a breather.' Conversely, one PRU/LSU manager noted that for some teachers being involved in an arts project could be quite stressful when it was outside their normal classroom experience.

> *Sometimes you can be actually quite exhausted because, if you are the maths teacher, it's very safe to teach a maths lesson because you know your ground, but when you are simply supervising kids in a whole totally different environment, totally different activity, you may not have to do anything at all, but you are anticipating what you might have to do and so it can actually be quite draining* (teacher, PRU project).

In one project, artists and other significant participants particularly highlighted stress as an outcome for the teachers involved, but this was believed to be part of a much wider issue within the teachers' professional lives rather than a direct result of their involvement in the project.

3.2.4 New or increased awareness

As with other studies of the effectiveness of arts education, two types of new or increased awareness for PRU/LSU staff were identified: awareness of the art form involved and of their pupils.

Most often cited was teachers' awareness of the potential of arts-based projects for working with pupils displaying challenging behaviour. Teachers referred to their not having been aware of what was available before, 'I didn't know there were people who could come in and do that', and to having gained an insight into what such organisations could achieve: 'It's certainly opened our eyes up. It's shown us that there are lots of things out there that we could do and work with.' In one project a negative impact in terms of awareness was noted in that the teacher involved had hoped that the cultural context of the art form would have been explored more fully, whereas the focus was perceived to have been on completing the tasks.

Recognising the potential of arts-based projects appeared to be inextricably linked with a greater awareness of the pupils and what they could achieve, 'seeing the kids in a different light', as they interacted with other adults and 'recognising other aspects of their characters and their potential'.

For staff in one project a residential element had been 'hugely beneficial' in this way.

> *Instead of seeing this young person 9.00 am to 3.30 pm they are actually dealing with this young person – chilling, eating food with them of an evening, and then when you come back to school, the way you are thinking about that young person is quite refreshed* (artist, LSU project).

As well as PRU/LSU staff seeing pupils in a different light, pupils also had the opportunity to view their teachers differently: 'It lets the pupils see a fresh side of the teachers that they work with on a daily basis.'

3.2.5 Attitudinal and motivational outcomes

For a number of PRU/LSU staff, their new or increased awareness had led to changes in attitude, both towards the pupils and towards the role of the arts in teaching challenging young people. In other cases it had reaffirmed attitudes that had perhaps become a little jaded within the current educational climate: 'It sort of reminded you what teaching was all about.'

Artists also noted that greater awareness and/or changes in attitude had resulted in teachers being more willing to become involved in similar projects or approaches with the young people.

> *They are more willing to try slightly different things to get to those certain kids* (artist, PRU project).

> *It is the interest and the thought if they can be good there then maybe we could try this, that and the other – that's where you gain* (artist, PRU project).

However, for some, enthusiasm and motivation to repeat the experience was tempered with a certain wariness which came from the knowledge of exactly what was involved in terms of setting up and implementing the project: 'It was incredibly time consuming.' That said, the same staff reported that they would encourage others to do it and that they could usefully inform others of the potential benefits and pitfalls of this type of work. For others, their motivation to take on a similar project was affected by the recognition that the opportunity was dependent on funding being available.

> *It did open our eyes to what was available but it always boils down to the fact that we have got no money and that we couldn't possibly afford to run or to buy that product in* (teacher, LSU project).

3.2.6 Informational outcomes

Involvement in the arts projects and the relationships they had built up with the artists was reported to have provided PRU/LSU staff with a network of contacts to approach in order to pursue future work in this area: 'We want to now find out what else there is, what else is available.'

3.3 Impact on artists

This section draws on data from the interviews conducted with artists and other significant participants, for example, individuals with specific (or specialist) knowledge, such as the head of an arts organisation, cultural venue or training organisation. It considers the impact on artists, particularly on their own practice as well as, where relevant, on their or other organisations, of being involved in the arts projects operating within the seven PRUs and LSUs.

3.3.1 Impact on practice

Perhaps unsurprisingly, artists were less likely to refer to any impact on their knowledge of the art form or artistic skills, although one did refer to learning to do certain tasks very quickly, for example editing, because of the limited attention span of some of the pupils, something that had then benefited the arts organisation in their everyday work. In one PRU a freelance artist and musician had worked in partnership, which had meant becoming more involved with the other's art form. As a result, the freelance artist reported gaining some music skills, albeit at a limited level. Another artist spoke of how the willingness of the young people involved in the workshops to try new things had impacted positively on his/her own creativity. However, s/he offered the caveat that it was necessary to balance the amount of workshops undertaken because they were quite draining and so could limit opportunities to pursue one's own art, which, in turn, could lead to creativity becoming 'a little stunted'. A sense of apprehension was voiced in one or two cases about exposing their art form to the potential negativity, or ridicule, of such challenging young people. However, this had been dissipated as the projects progressed and relationships were forged, and by what the young people had produced, what had 'blossomed' from their hands.

The majority of responses relating to artists' practice focused on their teaching skills and how the experience had enhanced their expertise in the dual role of artist/teacher, particularly where challenging behaviour was concerned. Involvement in the arts project was said to have provided an opportunity for artists to reflect on their practice and identify how they might improve it, or build on the experience in the future.

Enhancement of teaching skills

- *If anything I probably questioned my teaching techniques with those sorts of young people ... not to assume that everyone has an understanding of a certain thing.*
- *At the time I didn't think it probably enhanced my teaching skills but, in retrospect, I think it's experience for the future.*

- *It's had an effect on how I would approach other projects like this ... you learn from one thing and apply that to another. It helps in working out good strategies for teaching.*
- *We are actor/teachers, not just actors, not just teachers, and there is a real forging of the two together. That is our expertise and it is so needed in schools and PRUs, because what they get out of it is immense, and what we get out of it is, because we are learning all the time.*

Artists spoke of the importance of tailoring their teaching style to the group with which they were working. Two artists in particular recognised a need to be more flexible, especially in their approach to session planning, and to set more realistic boundaries: 'I think it's very easy when you plan something on paper to think a lot more will be achieved than actually can be.' In another project the need to provide a wider range of activities was highlighted. The capacity of the young people involved to concentrate for any length of time was found to have been underestimated, which consequently made managing their behaviour even more problematic.

Finally, a number of artists reported learning a great deal about implementing and managing such a project, 'it was a kind of naivety', which had led to a determination to do it better in the future. Issues highlighted were greater knowledge of the pupils involved and a deeper engagement with them in order to create 'a more meaningful learning experience', rather than thinking that a short or one-off experience was likely to be a panacea for everything or 'to change the world'.

3.3.2 Other impacts

A number of other outcomes for artists/arts organisations were highlighted, including:

- new or increased awareness (e.g. of the young people involved);
- attitudinal and motivational outcomes;
- therapeutic and affective outcomes;
- informational outcomes (e.g. expanded contacts/networks).

The opportunity to work with a different group, i.e. vulnerable young people, was highlighted in all but one of the arts projects, together with a new or increased awareness for artists of that particular group: 'It opened my eyes.'

New or increased awareness

- *It was the first time I had gone into a PRU, and just working within that context ... cleared all preconceptions I had... So on that level, every group of children you work with opens your mind a little more.*
- *I have never had experience with a PRU before so it has opened me up and given me knowledge of all of that.*

This awareness had led to more understanding of the issues affecting the young people and thus to an attitudinal shift, i.e. greater tolerance, as well as to an increased motivation to do more of the same work: 'If I had a reticence to do it beforehand, it's not there now.' One artist, who had found the experience particularly difficult because of relationship problems (both with PRU/LSU staff and subsequently with the pupils), had gone on to run some workshops for young offenders (set up by the same arts organisation) who displayed even more problematic behaviour. Interviewees, including the artist, felt that s/he had been able to use the experience positively by putting into practice what s/he had learnt from working with the PRU/LSU pupils on the project.

Artists also described therapeutic or affective impacts. Despite the fact that several of the artists had found working with this particular group of young people challenging, and in some cases stressful, the majority noted how rewarding the work had been and how much they had enjoyed being involved.

Therapeutic and affective outcomes: enjoyment

- *There was a buzz about the whole thing.*
- *On a personal level, you do get a good feeling … if you feel you are making a difference to these guys, then it can't be anything but a good thing.*

One artist highlighted the fact that, although individually each of the young people might have been challenging, his/her enjoyment had been enhanced because of working with such a small group, something not always possible when working in mainstream settings: 'It was actually such a pleasure to be able to work with a group where you could actually interact with them as individuals.'

There were references to the increased level of confidence to repeat the experience that artists now felt they had. This was particularly true for one of the arts organisations involved which had provided the venue for the project. Prior to becoming involved, staff had little or no experience of working with challenging young people, 'because nousey 14-year-olds don't come to [the venue] very much because they think it's really sort of boring'. The project had allayed many of their concerns and had left staff feeling much more confident about working with this particular group in the future.

Therapeutic and affective outcomes: confidence

- *It will help me in other projects because I will feel more relaxed when I go into another* [similar] *environment.*
- [They said] *how are we going to cope, what's it going to be like, so they all felt a lot more confident after the project, having seen and worked with these young people, to work with this group again.*

3.4 Impact on institutions

This section draws on data from interviews with PRU and LSU staff, artists and other significant participants to consider the impact of the arts projects on the institutions involved, i.e. the PRUs and LSUs (including the impact on their curriculum) and the arts organisations.

3.4.1 Impact on PRUs and LSUs

The impact of the arts projects on the PRUs and LSUs varied, although teachers were generally enthusiastic about changes within their institutions, for example, in terms of expanding the place of the arts within the curriculum. Both PRU and LSU staff felt that, in the short term, projects had enhanced the curriculum that these institutions were able to offer pupils, notably that projects had provided something additional to their everyday activities. Furthermore, in one PRU the arts project had in fact increased pupils' timetables where project activities were taught in addition to their core subjects.

Several interviewees spoke positively of the impact of projects on the institutions' overall enthusiasm and commitment to offer arts activities in the future, noting that they were keen to have an opportunity to become involved in further arts projects: 'I would jump at it.' At the time of the follow-up interviews one PRU was about to start another arts project with different artists and focusing on a different art form. This was noted as a specific response to the success of the arts project in the current study, 'because the kids have shown so much of an interest'.

However, some PRU/LSU staff identified a number of difficulties associated with the sustainability of future developments in the arts, most particularly resource constraints, which severely restricted their capacity for change. In one PRU project the demands associated with project organisation (for example, time and extra workload, providing staff cover and releasing pupils from the timetable) impinged on the enthusiasm and ability to repeat such projects. Unless time for effective planning was factored into the developmental stage of projects, and appropriately resourced, the projects' longer-term impact on the institutions was felt to be more limited: 'You might as well just throw the money down the drain to be quite honest.'

In spite of this, in several instances PRU and LSU staff referred to the impact of projects in terms of increasing their institutions' links with others, for example arts or cultural venues, which was regarded as being particularly useful for future joint work. In some cases the impact of projects on other teachers and professionals beyond the PRU/LSU was also identified as having implications for the institutions involved. For example, a teacher in one PRU noted that, as staff within the overall service became more aware of the positive impact of projects for pupils their support for future projects was likely to increase. In one LSU project, a member of the wider school staff who had been quite 'anti-arts', but who had some ability in the art form represented, had been so impressed with what the pupils had achieved that s/he was now collaborating with LSU staff to develop a school-wide club in that art form, 'a massive attitude change'. Sharing experiences and/or evaluations was also seen as a useful way of disseminating the potential of the arts projects beyond the confines of the PRU or LSU.

3.4.2 Impact on arts organisations

For arts organisations, the projects had impacted in terms of forging better links with schools and PRUs and, in some cases, creating new contacts, for example where freelance artists had been brought in to deliver the projects. One arts organisation was planning to work with partner organisations in order to offer more art forms, for example dance with drama, 'so the possibilities are endless really in terms of co-production stuff'. The head of another arts organisation spoke of the 'massive' impact that had resulted from their involvement in one of the projects. As a result of this and further work in PRUs the company was now involved in disseminating their experience to other organisations that might be considering working in this sector: 'We want to develop beyond direct impact between us and the kids as we think there is a big case to be heard which is not being heard.'

3.5 The legacy of the arts projects

A further consideration within the discussion of the impact of the arts projects on organisations is the legacy such projects leave. Interviewees affirmed that there had been a legacy for both the PRUs/LSUs and for the arts organisations involved.

When elaborating on the legacy for PRUs and LSUs, interviewees reiterated the enthusiasm of centre staff to repeat or extend the arts projects: 'It certainly pushes you to do more.' Artists believed that PRU/LSU staff were now convinced of the value of the arts for the young people concerned. As noted above, teachers proffered examples of PRUs and LSUs seeking to develop partnerships with other arts organisations in order to build on the success of the arts projects. In one PRU the teachers' enthusiasm had resulted in them funding further sessions with the same arts organisation, thus extending the project for the pupils. However, interviewees expressed some uncertainty regarding the longevity of this extension, with continuing funding cited as the main concern. Teachers referred to a legacy of increased skills and the confidence and experience to become involved in further arts projects. In one LSU any legacy was believed to have been dissipated because one of the two members of staff involved in the project had moved on, which had reduced opportunities to develop the work within school. In spite of this, the remaining staff member did affirm that, should further funding become available, s/he would certainly follow up any future possibilities to become involved in such projects.

Both teachers and artists described a physical legacy for the PRUs and LSUs in terms of the work left on display or the CDs and films that the pupils had produced. One artist referred to this as 'a library of imagery' – a positive representation of something the pupils had achieved to completion which would provide 'a constant good memory for them'. Pupils had learnt new skills in the art form represented and were now felt to recognise the importance of the arts. Teachers confirmed the pupils' enjoyment of the arts projects, 'they were all sort of like buzzing for about a week afterwards', and noted that they had been exposed to an experience that they would not usually encounter in their normal learning environment. This was said to have been a positive experience on which to 'reflect' and, for some pupils, it had represented a chance of 'a fresh start'. In addition, their exposure to arts organisations, and to the work of professional artists, was believed to have imbued pupils with a sense of 'connectedness' to the real world, in terms of thinking about their futures.

A 'learning' legacy was identified for arts organisations in terms of the desire, or 'definite wish', to repeat the experience, taking with them, as teachers noted, the lessons learnt from the current project: 'I think if we had structured it differently, it would have had a more profound impact.' For several artists and arts organisations, the legacy of the projects was described in terms of a greater awareness and understanding of the young people involved, which had encouraged them to want to do more of this type of work: 'We now know we can work with that age group.'

> The legacy is that our eyes have been opened to the local community a lot more…. It has made us want to rise to the challenge, because, at the end of the day, we really want to reach out to this local community, especially where there are a lot of disaffected young people (artist, PRU project).

Interestingly, for some artists the overall experience of being involved in the arts projects was considered to be as important as any legacy that they may or may not leave behind: 'It's a wonderful thing to do, just for the sake of doing it.' Moreover, one artist described how, in some instances, focusing on the legacy of a project might actually be 'binding', and indeed limiting, for future work, which might seek to rebuild that same legacy and, in so doing, hinder the development or 'evolution' of arts projects and their impacts.

Barriers to any legacy of the arts projects Although not probed specifically, a number of interviewees offered their perceptions of the barriers to maximising, or embedding, any legacy left by the arts projects.

The ever-changing nature of the pupil population, particularly within the PRUs, meant, for several interviewees, that physical legacies such as displays were often important in order to ensure any longer-term benefits. Once pupils were reintegrated or moved on, the longer-term benefits to them (e.g. success in their subsequent school career) were lost to the institution: 'We don't see the end product.'

However, the overarching barrier to building on any legacy of the arts projects was perceived to be the lack of sustained funding. The young people's enthusiasm for, and interest in, this form of learning experience was believed to have been stimulated and ongoing resourcing was thus felt to be necessary so that the impacts were not lost. Equally, the fluid nature of PRUs' and, to some extent, LSUs' clientele, highlighted above, meant that only one pupil group at any time was benefiting. In order to ensure equality of opportunity for other pupils, and to capitalise on the raised expectations of participating pupils, the importance of longer-term funding as opposed to one-off grants was again emphasised: 'To expect to have a massive impact on young people with a budget of £5,000, it ain't going to happen at the end of the day.'

Implications for policy and practice

- The array of impacts described offers great testimony to the benefits of arts projects for pupils' educational, social and personal development. However, interviewees recognised that time-limited arts projects were unlikely to have any profound effect on pupils' entrenched problems.
- Although the extent to which projects generate learning outcomes for pupils might be questioned, the value of enjoyment in pupils' learning should perhaps be acknowledged in itself.
- The benefits, both in the shorter and longer term, of projects as a 'positive shared experience' between teachers and pupils and the effect of this on the teacher–pupil relationship should not be overlooked.
- The value of other professionals working with pupils in PRUs/LSUs and the use of external arts venues as alternative locations for learning has been evidenced in the current study and might usefully be extended.
- The extent to which teachers were involved as hands-on participants in the projects, rather than in supportive or behaviour management roles, would appear to affect both the development of their own knowledge and skills and their understanding of the projects' potential in terms of pupil outcomes.
- The legacy of the projects in terms of their impact on institutions' enthusiasm and commitment to repeat or extend the experience, and the opportunities they afforded to develop and/or increase appropriate contacts should be acknowledged.
- However, for the impact of the projects on all those involved (pupils, PRU/LSU staff and the institutions) to be sustained in the longer term, both through future participation and/or to reinforce the experience of the arts projects, funding beyond one-off grants would appear to be crucial.

4 Effectiveness

This chapter focuses on the effectiveness of the different arts projects, drawing on the perceptions of artists, other significant participants, teachers and pupils of the main factors affecting the impact of the different arts projects. It considers:

■ the **key factors** or components affecting the impact of the arts projects;

■ the **distinctive contribution** of the arts and artists to that impact (in so doing, the chapter addresses the second of the study's main aims, see p. 16);

■ the **costs and cost-effectiveness** of the projects in relation to the impacts described in Chapter 3.

4.1 Factors affecting impact

A wide range of factors affecting the impact of the arts projects was identified. Whilst recognising some degree of overlap, these have been grouped into six broad types:

■ pupils
■ artists
■ teachers
■ relationships
■ projects
■ institutions

These categories and the variants within each are set out in Figure 4.1 overleaf and then discussed in turn.

4.1.1 Pupils

Pupils noted that their familiarity with the arts in general or with the particular art form in question affected their enjoyment of the project. For example,

Figure 4.1   **Factors affecting impact**

Pupils	familiarity with art form preference for learning style group composition/dynamics behaviour
Artists	background personality skills and pedagogy
Teachers	familiarity with art form pedagogy behaviour management
Relationships	artist–pupil artist–teacher pupil–pupil
Projects	planning content and relevance venue timing end product follow on
Institutions	place of the arts within PRU/LSU issues funding

those that already had some skill or had a personal interest in the art forms represented were more likely to feel that their involvement in the project had been beneficial. As one pupil noted: 'Well, I really like [break-dancing] so I reckon it's really, really good.' While a pupil from a different project who professed it to be 'boring' asserted this was because: 'I don't like playing music and I don't like playing instruments.' PRU/LSU staff supported this view, commenting that pupils who were interested in the art form were likely to be more motivated or enthusiastic about the project, certainly in the early stages. One of the artists noted that for those studying the art form, for example music at GCSE, being able to talk to someone who was actually making their living as a musician had been very useful.

A number of pupils referred to their preference for more practical or creative activities: they felt they had got more out of the activity because it suited their particular learning style. The effectiveness of a more flexible and informal approach to working with vulnerable pupils was highlighted in a recent study of LSUs (Wilkin *et al.*, 2003). As one pupil in the current study observed:

> *I'm not really an academic student. I'm more of a person who likes to be doing stuff anyway, a hands-on person – I'm not really a sit behind a desk and write for an hour sort of person, I have to be doing something … so I found it nicer if anything* (pupil, LSU project).

Other pupils also commented on the kinaesthetic element of the projects (i.e. learning through active, practical participation), noting that the fact that they were actually doing things, rather than writing about them, made the experience more enjoyable and thus more beneficial for them. Both PRU/LSU staff and artists highlighted the capacity of the arts to provide a positive learning experience for disaffected pupils. The practical nature of many of the activities was viewed as a means of re-engaging them in learning. For example, those who had difficulty with literacy and numeracy often met with a sense of failure in school, and what they could achieve then became limited in some teachers' minds. However, many such pupils were believed to have unrecognised talents that the more creative aspect of the arts could bring to light, thus raising their self-esteem and giving them a sense of achievement. Artists in particular spoke of how quite often the young people themselves did not recognise that what they were doing was creative, for example taking clothes apart and recreating them as a different garment, or putting decorations in their hair.

> *They really are highly skilled, but they wouldn't call it craft. They would do it all at home. It's not something that's part of school, therefore they don't quite see it in that context. But it's something they are doing and they are obviously enjoying and they are obviously very good at* (arts education development coordinator, LSU project).

> *They get up at half six, these kids who are being told they don't want to come to school and have got no motivation. She gets up at half six to do her face and make-up every morning, that is her means of being creative* (artist, LSU project).

The projects were then said to provide a means of tapping into that creativity and raising expectations of what the young people could achieve.

Both PRU/LSU staff and artists recognised that the composition of the group of pupils was often a significant factor in the projects' success. Artists in particular found that in some cases having too large a group made things difficult; in others a lack of consistency over which pupils attended each week was problematic. For example, in one PRU, attending the venue where the project took place was used as a reward for good behaviour. This meant that those who misbehaved during the intervening period could be prevented from returning the following week and sometimes substitutions were made.

> *It was hard for us because the group we had the week before and the group we were expecting the week after, half of them weren't there and they would replace them with other people* (artist, PRU project).

The behaviour of the pupils and the management of that behaviour sometimes posed problems for the artists, although those that had worked with both PRU and LSU pupils did note that the behaviour of the latter was generally less difficult. Two heads/coordinators of arts organisations noted that, in hindsight, it might have been useful to have had some prior knowledge of the pupils, in terms of both their behaviour and their level of arts skills. LSU staff from one project highlighted the need for prior knowledge of the content of the project, which would then have affected the selection of the pupils. Pupils had been chosen by heads of year and thus their age and ability range had been quite wide. This had affected the dynamics of the group, as pupils had not always felt comfortable with each other when performing certain tasks. Pupils from other projects commented on this issue, asserting that only those who really wanted to take part should be involved.

> *I think it would be better if they were asked whether they wanted to do it before the money was awarded to the [PRU/LSU] because if it is awarded beforehand then they are forced to do it, because you have to use the money up, but if you ask if people want to do it first, then I reckon that would go better because they have decided they want to do it* (pupil, PRU project).

The effect of group dynamics was evident in a number of projects, particularly where performing arts, such as music, drama or dance, were the featured art form. Peer pressure was raised as a significant issue by both PRU/LSU staff and artists from one project where two groups of pupils from different PRUs had been mixed together at the arts venue. Artists felt that they had underestimated the social tensions between the two groups, which had led to a lot of antagonism and meant that those who wanted to learn were often intimidated by those who did not.

> *The peer pressure they were all under meant they didn't open up to the music as they maybe would have done on their own* (artist, PRU project).

4.1.2 Artists

The background and personality of the artists involved was felt to be a key factor in the success of the projects. Pupils' comments tended to refer primarily to liking the artists because they were 'different' or 'not boring'; PRU/LSU staff highlighted the fact that the artists were often child-centred and very much on the pupils' wavelength. In some cases, seeing that adults who themselves had perhaps not done well at school were successful artists had been particularly influential for pupils. As one artist noted: 'They can see that someone who was like them has actually achieved.' In this way the artists functioned as excellent role models for the young people. They were variously described by PRU/LSU staff as being 'hip and trendy' or as having plenty of 'street cred', which was believed to have engendered respect and led to a good response from pupils. The head of one arts organisation concurred:

> *He's hard, he's local and you know he's been that kid in a way, so he was an ideal person and they respected him* (head of arts organisation, PRU project).

Artists' skills and pedagogy were perceived to be important by all interviewees. Overall, the quality most frequently identified was informality. Pupils particularly appreciated the more relaxed approach, the fact that they were able to call the artists by their first names and that they could talk and move around during the sessions; several referred to the fact that the artists did not shout or 'moan' at them.

> *Letting us work together and all that and we could talk – being let loose if you know what I mean, whereas at school you all just sit there and listen* (pupil, LSU project).

> *I'm very much about first name basis or nick name. It's not about me being Sir, I'm just* [Name] (artist, LSU project).

Whilst appreciating the informality, interviewees also noted artists' ability to assert authority where necessary (e.g. in response to pupil behaviour or to 'get things back on track'). The importance of outlining and establishing boundaries at the outset was also identified as a key aspect of this approach, which ensured that all parties shared a common understanding of each other's roles and responsibilities.

> [It's a] *friendly approach and informal, but quite clear about the boundaries.* [The pupils] *knew where they stood* (teacher, PRU project).

> *I think the best approach with the youngsters is to be fairly relaxed and to be fairly informal, but to set boundaries so, whilst your approach might be relaxed, you have still got to be very clear who is in charge* (teacher, PRU project).

A number of the pupils identified feeling that their thoughts and ideas were listened to by the artists: 'If you have got points of view, they listen to it more, they kind of hear what you are saying and they like take it in and help you.' Artists themselves confirmed that their approach was pupil-led (encouraging and implementing pupils' creative input) and responsive to pupils' needs, in order to provide them with a sense of ownership: 'They have to feel that they're in control of where this is going.' Although relaxed, artists stressed that there was a sense of purpose about the sessions: 'It's play but it's serious play.' However, in one project, pupils identified feeling under pressure, commenting that the artist was too directing or 'controlling'.

> *You needed to get things done and* [the artist] *was always there to make sure you did it* (pupil, LSU project).

In spite of this, the pupils fully recognised the professional skills of the artist involved, asserting that s/he was 'good at their stuff' and knew 'what they were on about'.

I had 100 per cent respect for [the artist] *but it could have been less stressful at times in the way that* [the artist] *came across* (pupil, LSU project).

A number of teachers identified the nature and quality of artists' explanations as an important element of their teaching style: instruction, demonstration and guidance were identified as the key processes. One teacher referred to the artists' 'kinaesthetic' teaching approach and commended this in light of the pupils' preferred learning style. Pupils also spoke positively about artists' instruction and guidance, noting in particular their willingness to work through any challenges that the pupils were experiencing.

For some teachers, the artists' attitude towards pupils was identified as a key factor of their teaching style; their positive approach to working with the young people was especially commended. For one teacher, the artists' enthusiasm was a particularly significant aspect of their teaching approach which transferred to the pupils involved: 'They have come with their equipment, their expertise and the love of their particular subject, as it were, and that kind of enthusiasm has been carried over.' In another project PRU/LSU staff noted the 'gentle' and 'caring' approach of the artists.

Artists' use of language was an aspect of their teaching style highlighted by both PRU/LSU staff and pupils. One teacher in particular referred to the 'soft tones' used by artists when communicating with the pupils, and compared this to their normal classroom experience, which would often involve shouting. Pupils also spoke positively about the way in which artists addressed them, again noting their tendency to talk to them as opposed to shouting at them: 'They could talk to us a bit better than teachers I think … like not shouting at us and telling us to work.' The positive impact of this approach was noted by one pupil: 'I have done more work than I would have done with the teachers.'

4.1.3 Teachers

Artists noted that the PRU/LSU teachers' familiarity with the art form sometimes affected the degree to which they involved themselves in the activities. In one instance, the teacher observed that not being an artist had, in their opinion, hindered their understanding of the concept involved: 'It was too deep.' Interestingly, the teacher assumed that this would also be the case for the pupils who took part, something the artists refuted: 'I think [the pupils] were very aware of what they were experiencing and how they were engaging in it.'

In another project the artist and the PRU/LSU staff had differing views on the extent to which the latter should help the pupils. The teachers saw it as a team approach whereas the artist believed that the teachers were helping too much and solving all the problems for the pupils. The artist felt that a failure on both sides to communicate had exacerbated the situation and led to the teachers holding back when their help with aspects of the pupils' behaviour would have been appreciated. In a third case the artists believed that a heavy staff presence for behavioural reasons inhibited their relationship with the young people involved.

For some artists the fact that the PRU/LSU staff involved changed each week had been particularly problematic in terms of developing a working relationship. At the same time a lack of younger male teachers amongst the PRU/LSU staff was identified. The art form (break-dancing) was seen as being particularly male orientated and although one or two younger members of staff did participate the majority of the centre staff, who were female, felt less able to do so: 'I don't think if I joined in that would encourage them very much.' This diffidence was felt to have influenced the teachers' involvement in the activities, as well as their expectations of what could be achieved.

4.1.4 Relationships

Artist–pupil Perhaps unsurprisingly, the majority of interviewee comments on relationships focused on that between the artists and the pupils. Generally, interviewees felt that this relationship was strong, founded on mutual respect and trust. Pupils appreciated the fact that the artists seemed 'more like a friend you hang around with', 'a safe guy'. In one project pupils spoke particularly of feeling special because the artist had trusted them with some expensive equipment.

> *Most people, you know, most older people, they don't trust kids but he like trusts us, all of us, to use this and I like this personality* (pupil, LSU project).

An artist considered that gaining pupils' trust was a fundamental aspect of the relationship, from which respect and understanding between the two parties could develop.

> *I think the biggest part of teaching this sort of young person is the trust element … I think respect comes once you have actually got trust in the relationship. If they know that I'm being honest about what I am and where I come from and that they don't need to hide anything from me, you can get quite a good creative working relationship* (artist, LSU project).

PRU/LSU staff also noted the natural comradeship that existed between the artists and the pupils, commenting that although casual it was still respectful. Artists echoed these comments, variously describing the relationship between themselves and the pupils as 'natural' and 'informal': 'They come to view us as their mates when we're there.' In another case PRU/LSU staff described how pupils 'hero worshipped' the artist when back at school. Again, the importance of establishing the boundaries of this relationship was noted by one artist, who emphasised the value of a friendly but ultimately working relationship with pupils: 'I'll be your friend, but I'll not befriend you.'

Artists particularly commented on pupils' need to feel valued and for trust to be established in the relationship. One noted that interacting with the pupils on an individual level was important, 'so they're feeling that they're my centre of attention'. References were made to the sense of value pupils gained from being allowed to use the equipment or to have access to cultural venues and, as in one case, art collections.

> *I would say where young people felt valued and they had a value for the activity so their behaviour and their whole attitude towards it were very different from how their behaviour would be in school* (arts coordinator, LSU project).

In the majority of cases, interviewees felt that the relationship between the pupil and the artists was different from the normal relationship with adults that the pupils would experience in school (teacher–pupil). Most commonly, interviewees identified the different boundaries of the teacher–pupil and artist–pupil relationships, noting in particular the artists' capacity to develop a more informal and relaxed relationship with pupils than was possible for PRU/LSU staff.

> [The artists] *can allow themselves to have that little bit more relaxed intervention with the kids, whereas as teachers, we have to be sort of, you will do what I say* (teacher, PRU project).

It is also important to note, however, that a number of positive references were made to the relationship between the pupils and PRU/LSU staff. In the majority of cases, artists, teachers and pupils considered the teacher–pupil relationship to be good but recognised that pupils would often respond positively to somebody who could be seen to be detached from their normal daily routine: 'They are often quite a lot better with people who are not going to have to make them sit down and do maths and English the next day (teacher, PRU project).' Similarly, one artist acknowledged the 'newness' of his relationship with pupils as one of the main differences from the teacher–pupil relationship, noting that for this reason pupils were likely to regard him as a 'bit of a treat' during the project.

Artists were at pains to highlight the importance of the mutual respect that underpinned the artist–pupil relationship, pointing out that this was something that was not always present between pupils and teachers in schools.

> *One girl said it you know, she said 'If they don't give me respect I won't give them respect.' And actually, the way some of the teachers were speaking to them you think yeah, because actually they are not given the respect at all, so why would you expect a young child to give any* (artist, LSU project).

Previous research has highlighted this opportunity for young people to 'establish positive personal relationships with an adult who can model pro-social values' and offer them respect, as one of three 'basic tools of repair' in re-engaging disaffected young people (Kinder and Wilkin, 1998). References to the use of this particular tool as a prerequisite for the success of the projects in the current study were very evident in the discourse of the artists and pupils, and, to some degree, in that of the PRU/LSU staff involved.

There were, however, some difficulties in the relationship between the artist and the pupils in one project. The artist and members of other arts organisations involved felt this had been determined, and subsequently exacerbated, by a breakdown in the relationship between the artist and the PRU/LSU staff. This was believed to have resulted in the pupils then mimicking some of the negative behaviour being modelled by their teachers. The PRU/LSU staff also spoke of the 'horrible dynamic' between the adults, which was then recreated between the artist and the young people.

The pupils themselves were very articulate about the problems. Although they recognised the artist's skills in the art form and appreciated the more practical, creative elements of the activity, they were of the opinion that the difficulties in the artist–pupil relationship had arisen because the artist was unfamiliar with working with teenagers: 's/he didn't know how to talk to us'; 's/he wasn't very good at saying things in the right way'; 's/he wasn't used to young adults – talked to us like we were five years old'. Pupil comments reflected an awareness of the difficult artist–teacher dynamic, with some noting that they tended to listen more to their PRU/LSU teachers and one asserting that the teachers 'didn't get on' with the artist either. Yet, in spite of these negative comments, the pupils had all enjoyed participating in the project and, in most cases, remarked that they would like to be involved in something similar again. At the same time, staff from the arts organisations involved noted that initial concerns that the outcomes might have been adversely affected by the situation had proved unfounded, the work produced had been 'a credit to everybody' and the pupils were felt to have gained a lot from the project.

Artist–teacher With the exception of the project described above, most artists and PRU/LSU staff spoke positively of their relationship, with several stressing its collaborative nature, which had developed over time. In many cases, the relationship had involved joint decision-making and effective communication: 'We talked a lot.' Artists variously spoke of the PRU/LSU staff as being 'helpful', 'supportive' and 'flexible', willing to discuss any issues that arose.

The less positive artist–teacher relationship outlined above was described as 'tense', which resulted in a refusal to communicate by the end of the project and a 'lack of willingness on both sides to be particularly grown up about it'. Interviewees from the arts organisations felt that the difficulties were due to a personality clash, which became evident very early on in the life of the project: 'people don't always get on'; 'there was just something that perhaps didn't gel.' Both PRU/LSU staff and artists identified the lack of opportunities between the artist and the teachers for collaboration and planning in advance of the project as a factor in this.

One of the hiccups of the project is that s/he just didn't meet myself and [teacher] *first, so we couldn't work out a way of working together ... we needed to develop a way of working but we didn't* (teacher, LSU project).

Perhaps from the beginning it should have been clearer. We should have maybe had a session and all of us thought 'Right, what shall we do with this project and the children?' (artist, LSU project).

Planning was identified as 'a vital aspect' in the partnership between artist and teacher in a study of residencies in education (Dahl and Jones, 1990). Similarly, in a review of artists in schools, 'careful' planning was said to allow 'the maximum benefit to be derived from the artist–teacher partnership' (Oddie and Allen, 1998).

However, once again, in spite of concerns that the relationship might have impacted negatively on the outcomes of the project in the current study, both PRU/LSU staff and the artist professed themselves to be pleased with the quality of the work the young people produced. At the same time, it was felt by both parties that the lessons to be learnt from this project could be put to good use in the future.

Pupil–pupil Pupils referred to the opportunity the arts projects had provided to develop new or strengthen existing relationships with other pupils. In several cases they were interacting with pupils who were not part of their normal peer group.

It gives you a chance to talk to people like you don't normally talk to around school (pupil, LSU project).

It brings a closeness to all the pupils in the [PRU] *which isn't normally there* (pupil, PRU project).

4.1.5 Projects

Planning It is perhaps not surprising, given the discussion in the previous section on relationships and in Chapter 2 on project organisation, that effective planning emerged as a key factor in the success of the projects. Several PRU/LSU staff felt that more planning would have aided their understanding of the project and thus have benefited them in other stages of the setting-up process, for example in the selection of pupils, as well as in establishing shared expectations and positive artist–teacher relationships.

We didn't have that many planning meetings and, with hindsight, we would have picked different children for the different workshops ... With the [previous arts organisations] *that I have worked with I have been able to see previews of the work they've done and you are able to match what you see with the group. This was very much blind* (teacher, LSU project).

We didn't meet the individual artists beforehand and, in hindsight, maybe that would have been more appropriate, so that the teachers supervising the session would have known what to expect (teacher, PRU project).

However, staff recognised that planning took time, an issue that was also highlighted by Oddie and Allen (1998) in their review of artists in schools. The authors observed that this should be factored into the early stages of projects and budgeted for accordingly.

Content and relevance The relevance of the project content or the art form represented emerged as an important factor. For example, art forms that were current and featured heavily in the daily lives of the young people, such as dance, 'that's cool', or music (especially DJ-ing which was seen as 'new and funky') had more relevance and thus more impact on them.

I think because it's street dance, it's break-dance, it's urban and it's where a lot of these kids are at right now in their lives, so it just makes sense for them and that's why it works here (artist, PRU project).

However, one of the female pupils in this project did note that the project's relevance for her had been diluted because of the lack of a female break dancer.

They should have a woman dance teacher because the men just teach break-dancing, … if there was a woman I would attend more because the boys just do break-dancing.

Relevance for pupils' own experiences was seen as key to their conceptual understanding of a drama project, which focused on a young person in 'desperate circumstances'. The pupils were able to empathise with the character and in reflecting on his/her experience were more articulate about their own, providing the artists with a greater insight into the pupils' lives.

Venue The effects (both positive and negative) of an outside venue for the arts projects were raised by PRU/LSU staff. On the positive side, it was seen as something exciting and different from the pupils' normal experience. For some emotionally damaged pupils where school was an element of that damage the opportunity to visit a different venue was seen as particularly beneficial: 'Anything positive that is outside school and is creative and could spark an interest must have an effect.' On the negative side, PRU/LSU staff felt that an outside venue could make things difficult in terms of managing behaviour: 'They could run around and hide.' Artists observed that sometimes teachers used to working within school systems found it hard to work outside them, especially in terms of setting boundaries for behaviour. The issue of transporting pupils to and from outside venues was also highlighted by centre staff.

Several artists referred to the positive effect of running the projects at an external venue. The head of one arts organisation identified the benefits of having the young people in and 'really using' the cultural venue, especially when it was one with which they were perhaps not very familiar, or which was not seen as being particularly trendy. In one project with an LSU the majority of the sessions had taken place at an outside venue. However, one session had been held back at the school because of logistical problems at the arts venue. The artist felt that this session had not been as effective because the pupils had been too distracted by school life: 'The young people kept going out of the sessions and they had all their other friends sort of distracting them, it was like being back at school again and it wasn't a special project.'

Timing Comments relating to timing as a factor in effectiveness tended to focus on the need to adjust this according to the circumstances of the pupils, e.g. making it full days instead of half days to maintain their concentration, or because of the logistics of having pupils out of school and arranging the transport.

> *I think it was 12 sessions and from my previous experience I cut that down to six sessions, as in six days rather than 12 half days, because half days don't work. By the time you've got them out, by the time you've got them back, you are actually inventing some kind of bus routine there, rather than actually doing the activity* (teacher, LSU project).

Other PRU/LSU staff comments related to the short-termism of the projects: 'I think if we could have gone on for another six weeks we would have really got there with them.' Pupils also highlighted this issue:

> *I would have liked it if we had done it a bit longer* (pupil, PRU project).

> *I remember needing more time to finish things off and to make it better because we didn't have a lot of time* (pupil, LSU project).

End product Although recognising the importance of the actual process itself, PRU/LSU staff in six of the projects did stress the value of an end product, whether that be a final performance, for example in a music or a dance project, or some sort of display, for example of artwork. Having something to show parents, other staff and pupils, and even the public in some instances, was seen as a way of providing feedback for the pupils on their achievement 'via a public medium' and as a powerful means of raising self-esteem and often of changing perceptions of this particular group of pupils.

> *They don't get any recognition really, they get so much negative – I think something like this is very positive, it's long-lasting and other people can see that they're not what people envisage them to be all the time* (teacher, PRU project).

In the seventh project, PRU/LSU staff noted that, although a conscious decision had been taken not to have a final performance, in case it had proved to be a barrier to the pupils' participation, this was something they planned to move towards in the future in light of the perceived success of the project.

Artists also highlighted the benefits of some sort of celebration or validation of the pupils' work, which provided a form of 'closure' to the project. In three projects that focused on visual arts, the fact that the pupils' work was put on public display was believed to be very important for the young people involved, it acted as a 'showcase' for what they had achieved.

> *It's a huge thing for these young people, because it is their work which has been chosen to represent the school, which is amazing and they need to understand that* (artist, LSU project).

In other projects, tangible evidence for the pupils of what had been achieved, such as making a CD of their music or putting the film they had made on to DVD and designing the cover, were seen as very important and much appreciated by the pupils.

There were some problems with the artwork to be displayed from one LSU project, which was taken back to the school prior to a session being held there and was accidentally put out for the rubbish by the cleaners. Although it had been possible to rescue the work, the artist spoke at length about how upset s/he had felt, commenting that s/he felt the event, and the teacher's apparent lack of compassion over what had happened, had given the impression that the pupils' efforts were not valued. This view was not supported in either the teacher's or the pupils' discourse and it may well be that the well-documented difficulties in the artist–teacher relationship had prevented any discussion and thus exacerbated an obviously stressful event for the artist. LSU staff and pupils referred to a feeling of pride in seeing the final display, which had been held at a cultural venue where the pupils' work was shown alongside the work of pupils from other projects.

> *The thing that stood out the most was the day we displayed everything.*
> *It was nice wandering around seeing what all the other groups had done,*
> *and they had had the same amount of time as us and seeing what they*
> *had achieved in that six weeks and seeing what we had achieved*
> (pupil, LSU project).

LSU staff noted that the fact that the event had been professionally organised, with an expensive buffet lunch, gave the work status: 'The whole thing said "We are going to value you" and I think they took that away.' References to the quality of the food featured quite highly in the pupils' accounts. The work had then remained on display back at the school for a period of time and some elements of it were in fact still being used, for example as props in school drama productions.

Follow-on Although interviewees were in agreement that the projects had achieved success and had, albeit to varying degrees, met their aims, a number did express the view that the impact would have been stronger with some element of follow-on. In some cases this had been prevented by a lack of funding beyond the life of the project grant, or because pupils, and sometimes staff, had moved on once the project ended.

> *What I don't like as an artist or as a workshop leader is that you achieve a body of work with the young people and at the end of that project, it is like 'OK, see you later, bye' and there is no sort of follow-on* (artist, LSU project).

4.1.6 Institutions

The value placed on the arts in the culture and ethos of the educational institutions involved was seen as crucial to the success of the projects. Where the role of the arts in providing a valuable learning experience for vulnerable young people was recognised, the institution was said to be more committed to supporting this type of work. Two of the LSUs in the current study were in schools that had either been awarded, or were in the process of applying for, specialist arts status and thus were seen to have a significant emphasis on the arts: 'They can really see the benefits of the arts.'

Internal struggles or difficulties within the schools were highlighted as a factor in determining the effectiveness of some of the LSU projects. Artists referred to having to absorb the conditions of the schools when setting up projects with LSUs, which functioned as microcosms of the whole, and how these conditions could affect the outcomes. For example, in one school a general lack of organisation, which delayed the start of the project, was attributed to the fact that several members of staff were leaving that year and the school was said to be 'in crisis'. An artist who had worked in both PRUs and LSUs commented that it was easier in PRUs, being smaller, to ensure commitment and involvement in the arts project, as well as its place within the overall arts curriculum. In one of their PRU projects the head of art had been involved as the key member of staff so there had been greater continuity with the work the young people were doing within the centre.

It would appear that the relationship of the LSU with the school, as well as the extent to which it was embedded in the school ethos and culture, also affected the level of impact. One of the three LSUs in the current study was perceived by the staff to be an addition, 'bolted on', rather than an integral part of the school's support structures and thus the impact of the arts project was perhaps more limited. At a second LSU, although it was considered to be embedded in the school systems, staff had not had much contact with the project: 'They didn't pay a lot of attention to it to be honest.' Consequently, the impact of the project was perceived to have been confined to the LSU, although the arts organisation reported a follow-up booking for the wider school population. The artists at both of these LSU projects referred to wider school issues which they felt had affected the level of impact. In the third school, the LSU was viewed very much as 'part of the school' and was in fact physically located at its heart. The impact of this arts project was felt to be extensive, with the school putting its own money in to continue it, as well as planning changes to the school curriculum to include more visual arts and music lessons: 'What we are hoping to see is how the arts can impact on the whole-school curriculum as well.'

Funding was also identified as a factor affecting success; but this is discussed in more depth in Section 4.3.

4.2   The distinctive contribution of the arts and artists

I think any type of arts intervention for our type of student is imperative.
I think we need it more than anything, more than anything at all
(teacher, PRU project).

Interviewees in each of the seven projects were asked for their views on the role of the arts in re-engaging young people in education. In the follow-up phase of the research, interviewees from the three current projects were asked to elaborate on what they felt was particularly distinctive about the arts as opposed to activities of another nature, as well as what was distinctive about the artists and their teaching styles. This section draws on interviewees' responses to these questions.

4.2.1   The distinctive contribution of the arts

Comments relating to the distinctiveness of the arts focused essentially on the fact that they were different from pupils' normal learning experiences. Other perceptions of distinctiveness then clustered around the following closely related themes, that the arts:

- were of a practical rather than an academic nature;
- allowed pupils to achieve;
- were contemporary, 'part of their youth culture';
- allowed pupils to express themselves;
- developed the whole child.

The overarching sense of distinctiveness, identified by teachers, artists and pupils, was that the arts were different from the pupils' normal experience of learning: 'It's individual and so different.' The projects provided a situation with which the pupils were not familiar, and which was therefore somewhat 'unpredictable' in a milieu (i.e. the PRU or LSU/school) that was normally very structured and thus predetermined. Equally, the pupils were working with artists (often young themselves and able to 'speak to [the pupils] in their language') who were perceived as being very different, in terms of personality and approach, from their teachers. In five of the seven projects, the pupils were taken out of their normal learning environment to participate in activities at other locations, e.g. a museum, dance studio, music studio, or the local community, which in itself was a new experience. The significance of location has been identified in previous NFER research in terms of enhanced learning outcomes (Downing *et al.*, 2004). Although the positive effect of an outside venue was recognised in the current study (see the earlier discussion on key factors in this chapter), this issue was not raised specifically in terms of what made the arts distinctive.

The practical 'hands-on' nature of the activities was identified by teachers and artists as being a particularly distinctive element of the arts: 'It's not writing.' This element was felt to be attractive to the young people attending the PRUs and LSUs, many of whom were said to find academic areas of the curriculum difficult.

> *I think it's a really, really good way of doing things, because a lot of children that we find here aren't academic, so anything that they can get their hands on and do arty things, or make things, they enjoy that more* (artist, PRU project).

Most importantly, developing the kinaesthetic side of pupils' learning was believed to allow the pupils to achieve, when previously they had experienced mainly failure.

> *It's the sort of thing these kids need. They've failed in other ways and they haven't got the support that some of us have got at home and, from that angle, they can do their own thing and produce something that they are proud of* (teacher, PRU project).

> *Through* [this work] *they can explore the world of possibility rather than the actual which is what they are dominated by. I think, in actuality, they are failures and they feel like failures. So this work is great. In this work they can explore solutions and they can own it – that's its great strength* (head of arts organisation, LSU project).

Teachers particularly appreciated the opportunity to see the pupils in a more positive light than was normally the case, and to praise their achievements: 'We tend not to always have a positive role, or say good things about them.'

For many, the arts represented a means of highlighting previously unrecognised skills in pupils who perhaps had difficulties with literacy and numeracy and therefore struggled in certain lessons. At the same time, the fact that there was no assessment or examination at the end of the projects allowed the pupils to both engage and progress with the activity at their own level.

> *Often they are kids who have talents which lie elsewhere ... here they don't feel the same expectation and pressure that perhaps they might do in other subjects* (teacher, PRU project).

It was something that they could all meet on their own level, engage in on their own level and feel comfortable in, because there was no test at the end of it and everyone came out with a different product. There was no right or wrong, there wasn't an ideal that they all had to meet, so there were lots of ways they could enter into it, and they did (teacher, PRU project).

Although pupils themselves found it more difficult to articulate a sense of the distinctive contribution of the arts, their feeling of achievement was often evident in their accounts: 'It was good because I achieved something.' One pupil referred to the creation of a music CD as 'a once in a lifetime opportunity'.

Pupils' obvious interest in, and enjoyment of, the arts activities were believed to stem from the fact that the art forms were often very current, featuring strongly in their everyday lives, and thus pupils could relate to them: 'It's modern and they're into that, it's part of their youth culture.' There was a feeling that, as such, the arts activities had a better image than other activities of a different nature and, as a result, pupils would 'go along' with them more. This was believed to have particular relevance for more challenging pupils.

When there is a focus and they are enjoying it, something like music and DJ-ing, creating it can actually make them forget about the problems that perhaps they have with people (teacher, PRU project).

I think it is a very important way of working with these young people, it doesn't matter how you are doing it, it is about tapping into what they are interested in. If you can find something that they are interested in and you can hold their attention span, you can hold them and their interest and their motivation, and then you can move them forward (teacher, PRU project).

The creative aspect of the arts was believed to be distinctive in that it allowed the young people to express themselves in more positive ways than through anger or aggression. Arts, in whatever form, were thought to help children to make sense of their world and express their feelings. One example given was the use of drama and role play, which enabled pupils to explore their own difficulties through another medium. The arts were also considered to allow young people to have an opinion about something and be 'passionate' about it, without fear of contradiction.

What I like about the arts is that there is no right and there is no wrong. If you can argue with me about why you want to take that picture, or paint that portrait, or put that pile of rubbish in the corner and call it art, if you have actually got an opinion about what you're trying to discuss with me, then yeah, it's art. That is why I think art works well with disruptive young people, because they can have an opinion that can only be challenged in a creative way – it could be done better (artist, LSU project).

Finally, the distinctiveness of the arts was described by teachers and artists in terms of developing the whole child, particularly their sense of self: 'The arts can help children define how they are now and how they want to be', and 'It actually brings across the essence of each young person that was involved.' Creating positive images of self through the arts emerged as a key theme in a recent evaluation of the Image and Identity scheme (Downing *et al.*, 2004), as well as in a study of the effects and effectiveness of arts education in secondary schools (Harland *et al.*, 2000). Interviewees in the current study also referred to the therapeutic, 'calming' effect of the arts, which was felt to be particularly important in working with more vulnerable or challenging groups of pupils. The 'transforming' effect of the arts on pupils' personal development, for example in raising self-esteem, building confidence and increasing social skills, was also highlighted. This then enabled the child to develop and grow (something that was also emphasised in the two studies referred to above).

> *For some of them, it actually exhilarated them and lifted them up out of the stupor or the tawdriness of everyday life and let them think about what they could possibly be – it let them dream* (teacher, LSU project).

4.2.2 The distinctive contribution of the artists

A number of factors have already been identified in section 4.1 as being key components of projects' successes, namely an artist's background, personality, skills and pedagogy. Comments relating specifically to the distinctive contribution of the artists reinforced these factors while focusing on three main areas:

- artists' high expectations of the pupils involved in the projects;
- enthusiasm for their art form;
- relationship with the pupils.

PRU/LSU staff commented on the high expectations that the artists had of the pupils involved in the projects, in terms both of what they could achieve and of their behaviour. The artists were said to have very high standards as well as clear objectives for each session so that the pupils understood what was expected of them. Although the approach was informal, PRU/LSU staff, as well as artists themselves, referred to 'a line' that the pupils knew they should not step over.

PRU/LSU staff particularly referred to the enthusiasm that the artists had for their art form, which was very evident in their approach to the pupils: 'S/he was just so enthusiastic about it and that came over.' In the majority of cases, this enthusiasm was believed to then encourage and motivate both the pupils and the teaching staff involved in the projects.

> *Then the fact that s/he can do all this dancing, they like that. And so then they will respond by trying to be the same as him/her* (teacher, PRU project).

S/he's enthusiastic about it. You know, s/he makes you see the need for the enthusiasm. So I suppose, in turn, it comes back and you're a bit more enthusiastic about what you're doing as well (teacher, PRU project).

The relationship that the artists had with the pupils was believed to be equally important and distinctive. PRU/LSU staff noted that this had grown more positive over time. Pupils were believed to feel more confident with the artists as the projects progressed and to trust them more, something identified as being quite significant, a 'big thing', for some of the pupils involved. Both centre staff and artists again highlighted the fact that the artist–pupil relationship was one built on mutual respect: 'You give respect, you get it back.' It was felt that artists were calmer in their approach, more 'laid back', and thus did not need to resort to shouting at the pupils, something the latter appreciated: 's/he doesn't nag'; 's/he's well chilled out'. PRU/LSU staff also commented on the fact that the artists could spend more time with the pupils and really listen to what they were saying, then use the pupils' ideas as a basis for the workshop sessions. Pupils themselves reported that they had enjoyed the projects more and felt they had done more in the sessions because of the friendliness and more relaxed nature of the artists: 'S/he made it a joke, instead of "Right, we have to do this."'

4.3   Costs and cost-effectiveness

Each of the arts projects was funded, or part-funded, through a grant from the Calouste Gulbenkian Foundation, enabling the PRUs/LSUs to engage artists to work with their pupils. Interviewees were not always clear as to the amount of the grant awarded but generally it was reported to range from £2,500 to £5,000. One of the arts projects was part of a much bigger project involving two other educational establishments and various sources of funding (including the Foundation), and thus had a substantially larger budget. The majority of interviewees asserted that the funding had been appropriate, allowing them to run the projects as they had intended. As a PRU/LSU teacher noted: 'I was surprised at how much we got for the money.' However, there was some recognition that employing artists could be expensive, while one or two artists felt that the project could have been even better with more funding, for example in terms of making the activities more exciting, or providing some follow-on work: 'The budget does reflect the quality that you deliver.' Some PRU/LSU staff spoke of making contributions in terms of staff time, providing transport or making rooms available.

When asked to comment on the cost-effectiveness of the different arts projects, interviewees were unanimous in the belief that they were cost-effective. Perhaps unsurprisingly, given that the interview sample comprised people who were working on a daily basis with these vulnerable young people, the majority of comments relating to cost-effectiveness focused on the benefits for the young people themselves. Comments variously included the terms 'priceless', 'invaluable' and 'good value for money'. Although interviewees were fully cognisant of the fact that it was only a small number of pupils who stood to benefit, those benefits were recognised as potentially deep and sometimes far-reaching.

> *If you are actually targeting young people at risk and you are trying to make a difference, then I think we are talking about small numbers and probably lots of money ... but, in terms of cost-effectiveness, if you are actually looking at being able to turn a young person's life around, then it's very valuable to promote that approach* (head of arts organisation, LSU project).

> *The kids have got a lot out of it and I think the pleasure we have seen has been quite measurable – whether it is lasting, whether it changes them as an individual, whether it makes them a better person, a more compliant person I couldn't say, but I think the benefits certainly outweigh the costs* (teacher, PRU project).

One artist and the head of an arts organisation stressed the longer-term benefits beyond the life of the projects in terms of the savings to society in general, for example the costs that might otherwise be incurred as a result of offending behaviour.

> *If you think about kids only being in PRUs until 12 pm and then going out in the community and causing thousands of pounds of damage, well for that money, you could have had them in here every day, every afternoon, kept them engaged in something useful and they wouldn't go out and do it again. So yeah, it's incredibly cost-effective* (head of arts organisation, LSU project).

> *For three hours the [artist] is £100. To put one person in prison costs £300 a day. I think they have gained so much out of it that it will have inspired them not to go down that route and that they have the ability and the skills to do other things than stealing, or getting into drugs, or whatever. I see that as the big positive thing, hopefully it will let them feel that they have a chance* (head of arts organisation, PRU project).

It was recognised that although many of the benefits for the young people, such as improved self-esteem and confidence, were difficult to measure, their value should not be under-estimated. Several PRU/LSU staff and artists voiced the need for funding to be ongoing rather than via one-off grants, 'keep it going, give us more money', in order to effect any long-term change.

Implications for policy and practice

- It is worth reiterating that the importance of factoring planning into the early stages of projects, in terms of establishing both shared expectations and positive relationships, and of budgeting for this should not be under-estimated.

- Is the value of enjoyment in pupils' learning fully recognised? Given the Government's commitment to enjoyment and its emphasis within the seven arts projects in the current study, should it be more widely acknowledged throughout the education community as an important factor influencing effective learning?

- Equally, given the current development of the 14–19 learning landscape, with the introduction of greater vocational opportunities, might there also be scope for building on the more practical, kinaesthetic learning style of arts projects?

- It should also not be overlooked that the current study gives evidence of the value of providing opportunities for pupils to 'establish positive personal relationships with an adult who can model pro-social values' (Kinder and Wilkin, 1998).

- Although employing artists was perceived as fairly expensive, the projects were considered to be valuable by all parties: pupils, artists, teachers and institutions. Comments showed a belief in the cost-effectiveness of the provision, in terms of benefits to the pupils themselves, but also in terms of add-on benefits for the PRU/schools in the development of expertise within the wider institution. This highlights, once again, the significance of appropriate resourcing beyond one-off grants.

5 Concluding comments

This study has examined the effects and effectiveness of arts activities in PRUs and LSUs in order to provide robust evidence for the value of funding such activities in the future. Although it is small in scale, and the projects relatively short-term, the study identifies very evident effects, for both individuals and institutions, of being involved in the arts-based projects under consideration here. These can include:

for pupils
- increased knowledge and skills in the particular art form;
- improved listening and communication skills and ability to interact within a group setting;
- increased confidence and self-esteem, leading to positive changes in behaviour;
- the 'buzz' of participating; pupils gained a sense of achievement, satisfaction and, above all, enjoyment from the projects;

for teachers
- improved knowledge and skills in the particular art form;
- an impact on general classroom practice, e.g. using demonstration rather than instruction; new approaches to managing challenging behaviour; including the arts in their own lessons;
- higher expectations of their pupils;

for artists
- the development of specific teaching skills, particularly a dual artist/teacher role;
- more understanding of the issues and needs of the client group;
- an enthusiasm for future work in this area.

The study's findings show the positive contribution that arts-based projects can make to the educational, social and personal development of disaffected and challenging young people, at least in the short term. The cameos and comments included in the report offer eloquent testimony to the potential significance of these projects for such pupils' re-engagement with learning. The study also demonstrates that the contribution of arts-based projects is distinctive in that they are: practical rather than academic; contemporary and relevant to pupils' own interests; allow pupils to achieve, when previously they had experienced mainly failure, and to express themselves more positively; and focus on developing the whole child, particularly his/her sense of self. They also provide examples of how education can be made enjoyable; an ideal to which the current Government remains committed.

The report highlights how central the presence and role of the outsider – the artist – is in the success of such projects. Pupils respected the artists because they were seen as experts coming in from the outside world and as being on their wavelength. The pupils responded to the artists' more relaxed and informal approach to teaching; their positive attitude towards the pupils; and their willingness to listen to pupils' ideas. The effects of the projects on the PRU/LSU staff also show how the presence of an artist with fresh skills, ideas and attitudes can inform general teaching practice both beyond the life of the project and in other curriculum areas. It is not surprising, therefore, that, for PRUs/LSUs and for arts organisations, the legacy left from participation in these projects was a real enthusiasm for further participation and that interviewees were unanimous in their belief in the cost-effectiveness of the provision.

However, the findings do not provide any strong evidence to suggest that short-term arts experiences have a lasting influence on these young people's lives and life chances. In order to investigate fully the potential contribution of arts activities to the social inclusion agenda, these activities would need to be a sustained component of the curriculum. Moreover, the report raises the concern that, without a commitment to longer-term funding from whatever source and/or investment by the school or PRU, the sustainability of positive outcomes is in question. Further, a number of key factors in successful projects, for example, providing the time for planning and efficient administration, taking pupils to external venues, ensuring a 'showcase' end product, all have substantial cost implications.

The study identifies flexibility on the part of both artists and teachers as another important component of successful projects. The findings demonstrate that the success of these arts interventions occurs not just where funding is sufficient and/or sustained, but also where there is a greater degree of commitment to collaboration and change. This has obvious implications for both teachers and artists in terms of the pedagogical skills they may need to develop in order to fulfil their respective roles. It also has wider implications as a new landscape of partnership-working takes shape in our statutory services and in the arts. Partners will need to be responsive and adaptable in order to engage effectively with different professional cultures and their discourses.

Partnership-working may also hold important opportunities for those organisations committed to funding arts initiatives with a view to improving social inclusion. As the current national agenda and policy around *Every Child Matters* (HM Treasury, 2003) and the *Children Bill* (2004) reshape services and roles, direct involvement with the strategic partnerships and youth forums being developed by our local authorities could be a valuable way forward.

In conclusion, this study has demonstrated the significant short-term effects that can be achieved in PRUs and LSUs through participation in short-term arts projects funded by relatively small amounts of money. It begs the question as to what might be possible if more sustained funding or a more permanent place for arts activities within the PRU/LSU curriculum is made available.

References

COLLINS, M.F., HENRY, I.P., HOULIHAN, B. and BULLER, J. (1999). *Research Report: Sport and social exclusion. Policy Action Team 10: A Report to the Department for Culture, Media and Sport.* London: DCMS.

DAHL, D. and JONES, S., eds (1990). *Residencies in Education: Setting them up and making them work.* Sunderland: AN Publications.

DEPARTMENT FOR EDUCATION AND SKILLS (2002). *Revised Guidance on Exclusion From School: Draft for consultation.* London: DfES.

DEPARTMENT FOR EDUCATION AND SKILLS (2003). *Excellence and Enjoyment: A strategy for primary schools.* London: DfES.

DOWNING, D., JONES, M. and KINDER, K. (2004). *'A good image of myself': An evaluation of the image and identity scheme.* Online: http://www.nfer.ac.uk/research/downloads/VADReport.pdf

HARLAND, J. and KINDER, K., (1997). 'Teachers' Continuing Professional Development: Framing a model of outcomes'. *British Journal of In-service Education,* 23, 1, 71–84.

HARLAND, J., KINDER, K., LORD, P., STOTT, A., SCHAGEN, I., HAYNES, J., CUSWORTH, L., WHITE, R. and PAOLA, R. (2000). *Arts Education in Secondary Schools: Effects and effectiveness.* Slough: NFER.

HAYDEN, C. (1997). *Children Excluded from Primary School: Debates, evidence, responses.* Buckingham: Open University Press.

HM TREASURY (2003). *Every Child Matters* (Cm. 5860). London: The Stationery Office.

HOUSE OF LORDS (2004). *Children Bill.* London: The Stationery Office.

INGS, R. (2002). *The Arts Included. Report of the first national conference on the role of the arts in Pupil Referral Units and Learning Support Units.* Calouste Gulbenkian Foundation and The Arts Council of England, Birmingham, 29 October 2001. Pershore: Nick Randell Associates.

KENDALL, S., KINDER, K., HALSEY, K., FLETCHER-MORGAN, C., WHITE, R. and BROWN, C. (2003). *An Evaluation of Alternative Education Initiatives* (Research Report No. 403). Norwich: DfES.

KINDER, K. and HARLAND, J. (2004) 'The arts and social inclusion: What's the evidence'. *Support for Learning,* 19, 2, 52–6.

KINDER, K. and WILKIN, A. (1998). *With all Respect: Reviewing disaffection strategies.* Slough: NFER.

KINDER, K., HALSEY, K., KENDALL, S., ATKINSON, M., MOOR, H., WILKIN, A., WHITE, R. and RIGBY, W. (2000). *Working Out Well: Effective provision for excluded pupils.* Slough: NFER.

ODDIE, D. and ALLEN, G. (1998). *Artists in Schools: A review.* London: The Stationery Office.

PARSONS, C. (1996). 'Permanent exclusions from schools in England in the 1990s: Trends, causes and responses'. *Children and Society,* 10, 3, 177–86.

RANDELL, N. (2002). *Including the Arts: Preventing youth offending. Report of the first national conference on the role of the arts in preventing youth offending.* The Paul Hamlyn Foundation, The Arts Council of England and the Youth Justice Board, London, 21 March 2002. Pershore: Nick Randell Associates.

WILKIN, A., HALL, M. and KINDER, K. (2003). *Learning Support Unit Strand Study* (Excellence in Cities Report 05/2003). Online: http://www.nfer.ac.uk/research/documents/EIC/05-2003.doc

Anne Wilkin, a Senior Research Officer with the Northern Office of NFER, has worked on projects involving research into pupil disaffection, family and adult literacy, special educational needs and professional development.

Caroline Gulliver, a Research Officer at the NFER's Northern Office, has contributed to studies on pupil disaffection and vulnerability, as well as school funding.

Kay Kinder is a Principal Research Officer and deputy head of the NFER's Northern Office. Formerly a primary teacher, she has extensive experience of research into pupil disaffection, the arts and professional development.